THE BIBLE
JESUS
READ

Resources by Philip Yancey

The Jesus I Never Knew
What's So Amazing About Grace?
The Bible Jesus Read
Reaching for the Invisible God
Where Is God When It Hurts?
Disappointment with God
The Student Bible, General Edition (with Tim Stafford)
Meet the Bible (with Brenda Quinn)
Church: Why Bother?
Finding God in Unexpected Places
I Was Just Wondering
Soul Survivor

Books by Philip Yancey and Dr. Paul Brand

Fearfully and Wonderfully Made
In His Image
The Gift of Pain

PHILIP YANCEY

THE BIBLE JESUS READ

ZONDERVAN™

GRAND RAPIDS, MICHIGAN 49530

The Bible Jesus Read
Copyright © 1999 by Philip D. Yancey

Requests for information should be addressed to:

Zondervan, *Grand Rapids, Michigan 49530*

Library of Congress Cataloging-in-Publication Data

Yancey, Philip.
    The Bible Jesus read / Philip Yancey.
       p.   cm.
    ISBN: 0-310-24566-4 (softcover)
    1. Bible. O.T.—Criticism, interpretation, etc. I. Title.
BS1171.2.Y36   1999
221.6—dc21   99-30791
                                                         CIP

Portions of Chapter 3 were published in *Destiny and Deliverance,* a collection of essays interpreting the life of Moses and the Dreamworks film *The Prince of Egypt.* Portions of other chapters appeared in different form in *Christianity Today* and *The Reformed Journal.*

Interior design by Sherri L. Hoffman

Printed in the United States of America

11 12 13 14 15 . 50 49 48 47 46 45 44 43 42 41 40 39 38 37 36 35 34

To Buck Hatch,
who first opened up to me
the delights and mysteries
of the Old Testament

CONTENTS

PREFACE

I feel a need to apologize for what you will *not* find in this book. Though I am writing about the Old Testament, "the Bible Jesus read," I feel neither qualified nor inclined to delve into such matters as author, date of composition, and the insights of literary or form criticism. I read the Bible as any ordinary reader does, interacting with the content, trying to understand the author's original intent. Because I make my living as a writer, I also peek "behind the curtain" to speculate why the author used a certain illustration, chose an unusual metaphor, or started here and not there.

After a chapter introducing the Old Testament as a whole, I have chosen a sampling from each of its major sections: history, prophets, poetry, and wisdom literature. Why these particular books? Oswald Chambers once said that the Psalms teach you how to pray; Job teaches you how to suffer; the Song of Solomon teaches you how to love; Proverbs teaches you how to live; and Ecclesiastes teaches you how to enjoy. I wish I had such sunny confidence in what I expect from the Bible! I'm afraid I made my selections—Job, Deuteronomy, Psalms, Ecclesiastes, Prophets—out of my own doubts and struggles, not because I expect these books to teach me the secrets of life. I find in these particular books companions for my pilgrimage. In them, I discover myself—and for this reason I have written about them personally and subjectively, not analytically.

I begin with Job because I have spent so much time in my own writing exploring Job's questions. Many scholars believe it to be the oldest recorded story in the Bible, a brilliant drama pre-dating even Abraham. Job strips a relationship with God to its bare essentials: one man alone, naked, having it out with his God. In a pattern that recurs throughout the Old Testament, God stacks the odds against himself in favor of human freedom, and the very fact that the Bible includes Job, with its powerful arguments against God's injustice, underscores that pattern.

Deuteronomy I chose because I love its tone of melancholy realism. While the rest of the Hebrews were itching to cross a river and enter the Promised Land, old man Moses took the time to reflect on the hard lessons they had learned and the harder ones they would soon face. The fact that we now use "crossing the Jordan" as an image of spiritual triumph shows that we have not yet absorbed the central message of this remarkable book. I wrote a different version of this chapter for a book to accompany the Dreamworks animation film *The Prince of Egypt*, which portrays the story of Moses and the Exodus. (In a few instances I followed their plot line, and added fictionalized detail to the biblical account.) Jewish readers of my manuscript were scandalized. Why this pessimism, this fatalism, this latent anti-Semitism in a work celebrating the grand miracle of the Exodus? In the margin beside some of the strongest passages a Jewish proofreader wrote, "Where is this from!?" I pointed out that each questionable quotation came directly from Deuteronomy, part of the sacred Torah.

I have always struggled to get past the baffling inconsistencies of the Psalms, and the best way I know to struggle is to write about whatever is bothering me. In the process, Psalms has moved from my list of "least favorite" books to "most favorite." In its chorus of voices, we hear every intonation of what getting along with God might involve.

How in the world did Ecclesiastes make it into the Bible? I have often wondered that, especially in periods when I identify so closely with the cynical viewpoint of its worldly author. And as for the Prophets, since childhood I have been "in recovery" from the homiletical abuse of those mysterious books. I write about them because I want to understand them.

∽∾

With some regret, I will avoid discussing many of the difficulties and stumbling blocks people encounter in the Old Testament. For example, it contains some six hundred passages of explicit violence, many of them linked directly to God himself. How do we reconcile that with the nonviolence preached by God's Son Jesus? I am tempted to drop everything and deal with these issues, but that would make for a very different book. This is not a book of argument or apology, rather, one of self-discovery. Besides, many authors far more qualified have taken up these issues in great detail.

Still, I must make two observations. First, I find the Old Testament to be, above all, *realistic*. When I view a play like *Macbeth* or *King Lear*, or a movie like *The Godfather* or *Saving Private Ryan*, I encounter a world of evil, violence, and revenge. I feel moved by those experiences because I recognize my world, violent in the playgrounds of Chicago as well as on the battlefields of Europe and Asia. Kids shoot each other at school, terrorists blow up airplanes and buildings, cops pound on handcuffed prisoners.

The Old Testament portrays the world as it is, no holds barred. In its pages you will find passionate stories of love and hate, blood-chilling stories of rape and dismemberment, matter-of-fact accounts of trafficking in slaves, honest tales of the high honor and cruel treachery of war. Nothing is neat and orderly. Spoiled brats like Solomon and Samson get supernatural gifts; a truly good man like Job gets catastrophe. As you encounter these disturbances, you may recoil against them or turn away from a God who had any part in them. The wonderful quality of the Old Testament is that it contains those very responses as well! God anticipates our objections and includes them in his sacred writing.

Kathleen Norris gives a healthy perspective on this issue in her book *Amazing Grace*:

> Many people these days feel an absence in their lives, expressed as an acute desire for "something more," a spiritual home, a community of faith. But when they try to read the Bible they end up throwing it across the room. To me, this seems encouraging, a good place to start, a sign of real engagement with the God who is revealed in Scripture. Others find it easy to dismiss the Bible out of hand, as negative, vengeful, violent. I can only hope that they are rejecting the violence-as-entertainment of movies and television on the same grounds, and that they say a prayer every time they pick up a daily newspaper or turn on CNN. In the context of real life, the Bible seems refreshingly whole, an honest reflection on humanity in relation to the sacred and the profane. I can't learn enough about it, but I also have to trust what little I know, and proceed, in faith, to seek God there.

Second, I detect in the Old Testament a gradual but certain movement toward grace. The Hebrews lived in wild, barbaric times. Their laws, which may seem harsh to us, represent a great softening compared to their neighbors' laws. They established basic rules of warfare and enshrined in their laws respect for the poor and care for the environment. They set limits on revenge and built Cities of Refuge. We must remember, as we look back on a time of blood-vengeance, slavery, polygamy, and contract marriage with a brother's wife, that God had to work with people's moral condition at its given stage. In the writings from this period lay the seed, but only the seed, of God's grace. "These are the Scriptures that testify about me,"

Jesus told the Torah-readers of his day, then added pointedly, "yet you refuse to come to me to have life."

"As nurses commonly do with infants, God is wont in a measure to 'lisp' when speaking to us," said John Calvin. In the Old Testament especially, God "lisped." Speaking in language that could be understood, God gradually edged his people toward a different way. He took the side of the oppressed and promised a Suffering Servant who would redeem not as the perpetrator but as the victim of violence. For a time he allowed behavior that he disapproved of, "because your hearts were hard." Meanwhile, albeit sometimes in zigzag fashion, the long vectors of history pointed steadily toward his Son, Jesus, the final revelation of God in human form. In Jesus, God no longer lisped; the Word spoke loud and clear.

I would like to explore these matters further, but not here. This is a book not of answers but of questions that I bring to the Old Testament, a set of writings as mystifying, infuriating, and strangely satisfying as life itself.

In our time, says one church historian, the social liberals have sought to recover the Gospels, the Pentecostals the book of Acts, and the evangelicals the Epistles. Perhaps we should join together ecumenically to recover the biblical books that preceded all of those. How easily we forget that the Bible's sweeping statements on divine inspiration ("All Scripture is God-breathed and is useful for teaching, rebuking, correcting and training in righteousness, so that the man of God may be thoroughly equipped for every good work" 2 Timothy 3:16–17) were written about the *Old* Testament, the only Bible these authors had.

ᏋᎥᎥᎥᎥᎤ

A warning: it may prove dangerous to get involved with the Bible. You approach it with a series of questions, and as you enter it you find the questions turned back upon you. King

David got swept up in a story by the prophet Nathan and leaped to his feet indignant—only to learn the barbed story concerned himself. I find something similar at work again and again as I read the Old Testament. I am thrown back on what I truly believe. I am forced to reexamine. Thomas Merton's words about the Bible in general apply to the Old Testament in particular:

> There is, in a word, nothing comfortable about the Bible—until we manage to get so used to it that we make it comfortable for ourselves.... Have we ceased to question the book and be questioned by it? Have we ceased to fight it? Then perhaps our reading is no longer serious.
>
> For most people, the understanding of the Bible is, and should be, a struggle: not merely to find meanings that can be looked up in books of reference, but to come to terms personally with the stark scandal and contradiction in the Bible itself....
>
> Let us not be too sure we know the Bible just because we have learned not to be astonished at it, just because we have learned not to have problems with it.
>
> —*Opening the Bible*

After spending time exploring the Old Testament, I can truthfully say that I come away more astonished, not less.

—Philip Yancey

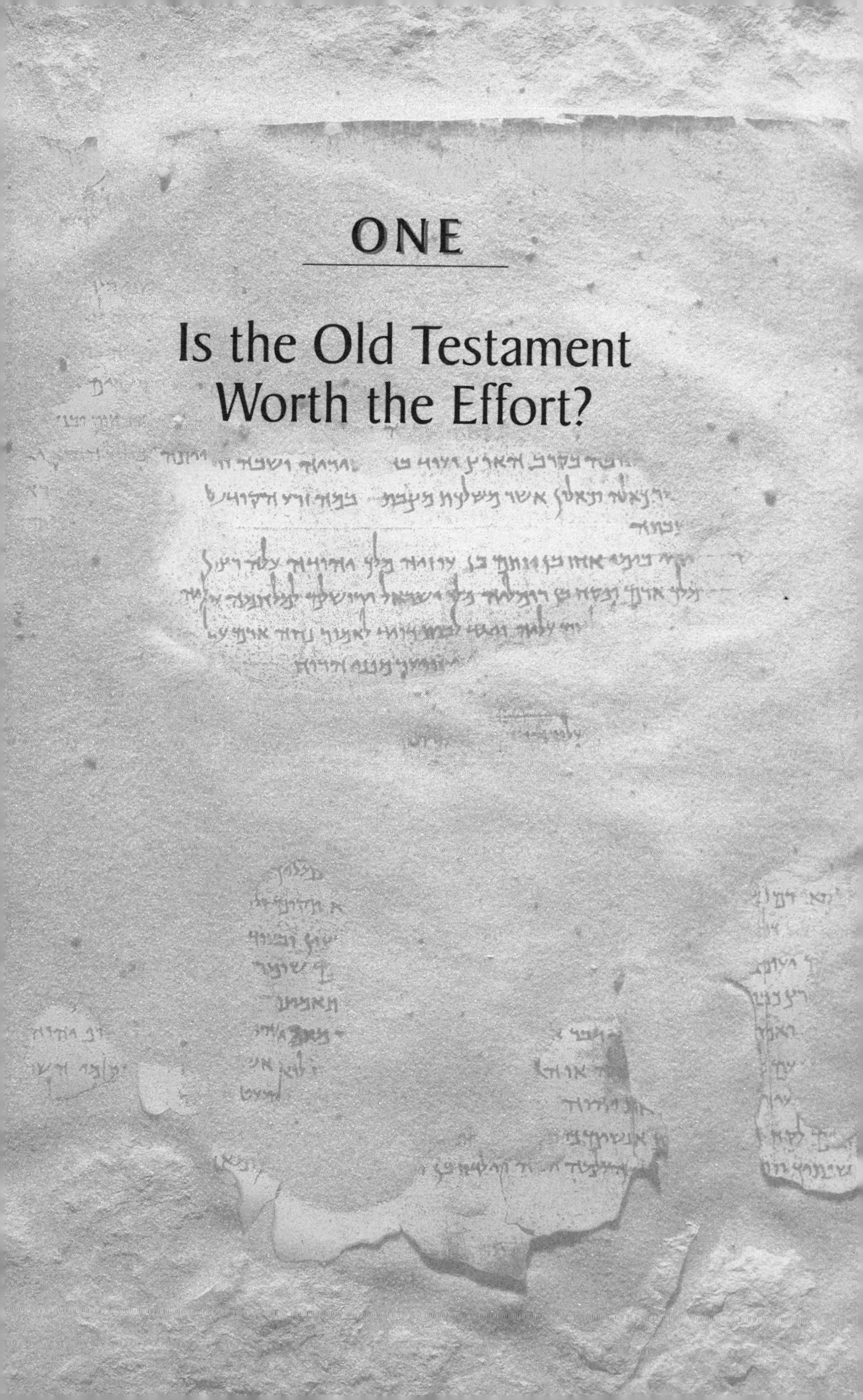

ONE

Is the Old Testament Worth the Effort?

ONE

Is the Old Testament Worth the Effort?

Faith is not the clinging to a shrine but an endless pilgrimage of the heart. Audacious longing, burning songs, daring thoughts, an impulse overwhelming the heart, usurping the mind—these are all a drive toward [loving the One] who rings our heart like a bell.

—ABRAHAM HESCHEL

My brother, who attended a Bible College during a smart-alecky phase in his life, enjoyed shocking groups of believers by sharing his "life verse." After listening to others quote pious phrases from Proverbs, Romans, or Ephesians, he would stand and with a perfectly straight face recite this verse very rapidly:

At Parbar westward, four at the causeway, and two at Parbar. 1 Chronicles 26:18.

Other students would screw up their faces and wonder what deep spiritual insight they were missing. Perhaps he was speaking another language?

If my brother felt in a particularly ornery mood, he would quote an alternative verse:

O daughter of Babylon ... Happy shall he be, that taketh and dasheth thy little ones against the stones. Psalm 137:9.

In his sassiness my brother had, quite ingeniously, identi-fied the two main barriers to reading the Old Testament: It doesn't always make sense, and what sense it does make offends modern ears. For these and other reasons the Old Tes-tament, three-fourths of the Bible, often goes unread.

As a result, knowledge of the Old Testament is fading fast among Christians and has virtually vanished in popular culture. In a comedy routine Jay Leno tested his audience's knowledge of the Bible by asking them to name one of the Ten Com-mandments. A hand shot up: "God helps those who help them-selves?" Everybody laughed, but no one else could do better. Polls show that eighty percent of Americans claim to believe in the Ten Commandments, but very few can name as many as four of them. Half of all adult Americans cannot identify the Bible's first book as Genesis. And fourteen percent identify Joan of Arc as Noah's wife.

More surprisingly, a Wheaton College professor named Gary Burge has found that ignorance of the Old Testament extends to the church as well. For several years Burge has been testing incoming freshman at his school, a premier evangelical institution. His surveys show that students who have attended Sunday School all their lives, have watched innumerable episodes of *VeggieTales*, and have listened to countless ser-mons, cannot identify basic facts about the Old Testament.

The experience of Barry Taylor, former rock musician and now pastor, suggests a reason. He told me, "In the early 1970s my best friend became a Jesus freak. I thought he was crazy, so I started searching the Bible in order to find arguments to refute him. For the life of me, I could not figure out why God was con-cerned with the bent wing of a dove, or why he would give an order to kill, say, 40,000 Amalekites. And who were the Amalekites anyway? Fortunately I kept reading, plowing through all the hard books. When I got to the New Testament, I couldn't find a way around Jesus. So I became a Jesus freak too."

I am glad Barry Taylor made it to Jesus, but I recognize that he raises some good questions in the process. Why does the Bible spend so much time on temples, priests, and rules governing sacrifices that no longer even exist? Why does God care about defective sacrificial animals—limping lambs and bent-winged doves—or about a young goat cooked in its mother's milk, and yet apparently not about people like the Amalekites? How can we make sense of the strange Old Testament, and how does it apply to our lives today? In short, is the Old Testament worth the effort it takes to read and understand it?

I have heard from missionaries in places like Africa and Afghanistan that people there respond immediately to the Old Testament, for its stories of land disputes, water rights, tribal feuds, and arranged marriages relate directly to how they live now. But such customs are far removed from a Greek-thinking sophisticate like the apostle Paul, and much further removed from the average suburbanite living, say, in Tampa, Florida. Those of us in developed countries who pick up the Old Testament and simply start reading may well feel boredom, confusion, or even outrage at the violence portrayed there. Jesus we identify with, the apostle Paul we think we understand, but what of those barbaric people living in the Middle East several thousand years ago? What to make of them?

Most people get around this dilemma by avoiding the Old Testament entirely. Or, perhaps worse, they mine it for a nugget of truth that can be extracted and held up to the light, like a diamond plucked from a vein of coal. That technique can backfire, however—remember my brother's life verses.

I can think of one ironic "advantage" to ignorance of the Old Testament. "The man of today ... must read the Scriptures as though they were something entirely unfamiliar, as though they had not been set before him ready-made," wrote the Jewish scholar Martin Buber. Buber is now getting his wish: most people of today *do* read the Old Testament as something entirely unfamiliar!

Why Bother?

This book recounts how I came to stop avoiding and start reading—ultimately loving—the Old Testament. I confess that I began with ignoble motives: I read it because I was paid to, as part of my editorial assignment to produce *The Student Bible*. Long after *The Student Bible* had been published and stocked on bookstore shelves, however, I kept returning to the Old Testament on my own.

My reading experience parallels one I had with William Shakespeare. In a moment of idealism, I made a New Year's resolution to read all thirty-eight of Shakespeare's plays in one year. Due to travel, a cross-country move, and other interruptions, I had to extend that deadline. Yet, to my surprise, fulfilling the task seemed far more like entertainment than like work. At first I had to look up archaic words, concentrate on keeping the characters straight, and adjust to the sheer awkwardness of reading plays. I found, though, that as I kept at it and got accustomed to the rhythm and language, these distractions faded and I felt myself being swept up in the play. Without fail I looked forward to the designated Shakespeare evenings.

I expected to learn about Shakespeare's world and the people who inhabited it. I found, though, that Shakespeare mainly taught me about *my* world. He endures as a playwright because of his genius in probing the hidden recesses of humanity, a skill that gives him appeal in places as varied as the United States, China, and Peru several centuries after his death. We find ourselves in his plays.

I went through precisely that same process in encountering the Old Testament. From initial resistance, I moved to a reluctant sense that I *ought* to read the neglected three-quarters of the Bible. As I worked past some of the barriers (much like learning to read Shakespeare), I came to feel a *need* to read, because of what it was teaching me. Eventually I found myself *wanting* to read those thirty-nine books, which were satisfying in me some hunger that nothing else had—not even, I must say, the New Testament. They taught me about Life with God: not how it is supposed to work, but how it actually does work.

The rewards offered by the Old Testament do not come easily, I admit. Learning to feel at home in its pages will take time and effort. All achievements—climbing mountains, mastering the guitar, competing in a triathlon—require a similar process of hard work; we persevere because we believe rewards will come.

A reader of the Old Testament confronts obstacles not present in other books. For example, I was put off at first by its disarray. The Old Testament does not read like a cohesive novel; it consists of poetry, history, sermons, and short stories written by various authors and mixed up together. In its time, of course, no one conceived of the Old Testament as one book. Each book had its own scroll, and a long book like Jeremiah would occupy a scroll twenty or thirty feet long. A Jewish person entering a synagogue would see stacks of scrolls, not a single book, and, aware of their differences, would choose accordingly. (Indeed, on certain solemn holidays Jews were only permitted to read from Job, Jeremiah, and Lamentations in order to stay appropriately mournful; the other books might provide too much pleasure.)

Yet I find it remarkable that this diverse collection of manuscripts written over a period of a millennium by several dozen authors possesses as much unity as it does. To appreciate this feat, imagine a book begun five hundred years before Columbus and just now completed. The Bible's striking unity is one strong sign that God directed its composition. By using a variety of authors and cultural situations, God developed a complete record of what he wants us to know; amazingly, the parts fit together in such a way that a single story does emerge.

The more I persevered, the more passages I came to understand. And the more I understood, the more I found myself in those passages. Even in a culture as secular as the United States, best-sellers such as *Care of the Soul* by Thomas Moore and *The Cloister Walk* by Kathleen Norris reveal a deep spiritual hunger. The Old Testament speaks to that hunger like no other book. It does not give us a lesson in theology, with abstract concepts neatly arranged in logical order. Quite the opposite: it gives an advanced course in Life with God, expressed in a style at once personal and passionate.

Neither Testament Is Enough

Christians of all stripes hold one thing in common: we believe the Old Testament is not enough. Jesus the Messiah came to introduce a "New Covenant," or New Testament, and following the apostle Paul we look back on the Old Testament period as a time of preparation. Without question I agree. Yet I am increasingly convinced that neither is the New Testament enough. On its own, it proves insufficient for understanding God or our world.

When Thomas Cahill wrote the book *The Gifts of the Jews* he chose the subtitle, "How a Tribe of Desert Nomads Changed the Way Everyone Thinks and Feels." He is surely right. Western civilization builds so directly on foundations laid in the Old Testament era that it would not otherwise make sense. As Cahill points out, the Jewish belief in monotheism gave us a Great Whole, a unified universe that can, as a product of one Creator, be studied and manipulated scientifically. Ironically, our technological modern world traces back to that tribe of desert nomads.

The Jews also gave us what Cahill calls the Conscience of the West, the belief that God expresses himself not primarily through outward show, but rather through the "still, small voice" of conscience. A God of love and compassion, he cares about all of his creatures, especially human beings created "in his own image," and he asks us to do the same. Every person on earth has inherent human dignity. Following that God, the Jews gave us a pattern for the great liberation movements of modern history, and for just laws to protect the weak and minorities and the oppressed.

According to Cahill, without the Jews,

> ... we would never have known the abolitionist movement, the prison-reform movement, the antiwar movement, the labor movement, the civil rights movement, the movements of indigenous and dispossessed peoples for their human rights, the antiapartheid movement in South Africa, the Solidarity movement in Poland, the free-speech and pro-democracy movements in such Far Eastern countries as South Korea, the Philippines, and even China.

So many of the concepts and words we use daily—new, individual, person, history, freedom, spirit, justice, time, faith, pilgrimage, revolution—derive from the Old Testament that we can hardly imagine the world and our place in it without relying on the Jewish heritage. A comic character in one of Molière's plays suddenly discovers, "I am speaking prose! I am speaking prose!" Similarly, our roots go so deep in Old Testament thinking that in many ways—human rights, government, the treatment of neighbors, our understanding of God—we are already speaking and thinking "Old Testament."

Most assuredly we cannot understand the New Testament apart from the Old. The proof is simple: try understanding Hebrews, Jude, or Revelation without any reference to Old Testament allusions or concepts. It cannot be done (which may explain why many modern Christians avoid those books too). The Gospels can be read as stand-alone stories, but a reader unacquainted with the Old Testament will miss many layers of richness in them. Paul constantly appealed to the Old Testament. Without exception, every New Testament author wrote about the new work of God on earth while looking through the prism of the earlier or "old" work.

A Chinese philosopher insisted on riding his mule backwards so that he would not be distracted by where he was going and could instead reflect on where he had been. The Bible works in somewhat the same way. The Epistles shed light backward on the events of the Gospels, so that we understand them in a new way. Epistles and Gospels both shed light backward on the Old Testament.

For centuries the phrase "as predicted by the prophets" was one of the most powerful influences on people coming to faith. Justin the Martyr credited his conversion to the impression made on him by the Old Testament's predictive accuracy. The brilliant French mathematician Blaise Pascal also cited fulfilled prophecies as one of the most important factors in his faith. Nowadays, few Christians read the prophets except in search of Ouija-board-like clues into the future. We have lost the Reformers' profound sense of unity between the two testaments.

Understanding our civilization and understanding the Bible may be important reasons for reading the Old Testament, but the title of this book hints at perhaps the most important reason: It is the Bible Jesus read. He traced in its passages every important fact about himself and his mission. He quoted from it to settle controversies with opponents such as the Pharisees, Sadducees, and Satan himself. The images—Lamb of God, shepherd, sign of Jonah, stone which the builders rejected—that Jesus used to define himself came straight from the pages of the Old Testament.

Once, a government tried to amputate the Old Testament from Christian Scriptures. The Nazis in Germany forbade study of this "Jewish book," and Old Testament scholarship disappeared from German seminaries and journals. In 1940, at the height of Nazi power, Dietrich Bonhoeffer defiantly published a book on Psalms and got slapped with a fine. In letters of appeal he argued convincingly that he was explicating the prayer book of Jesus Christ himself. Jesus quoted often from the Old Testament, Bonhoeffer noted, and never from any other book—even though the Hebrew canon had not been officially closed. Besides, much of the Old Testament explicitly or implicitly points to Jesus.

When we read the Old Testament, we read the Bible Jesus read and used. These are the prayers Jesus prayed, the poems he memorized, the songs he sang, the bedtime stories he heard as a child, the prophecies he pondered. He revered every "jot and tittle" of the Hebrew Scriptures. The more we comprehend the Old Testament, the more we comprehend Jesus. Said Martin Luther, "the Old Testament is a testamental letter of Christ, which he caused to be opened after his death and read and proclaimed everywhere through the Gospel."

In a poignant passage from his Gospel, Luke tells of Jesus spontaneously appearing by the side of two disciples on the road to Emmaus. Even though rumors of the Resurrection were spreading like wildfire, clearly these two did not yet believe, as Jesus could tell by looking into their downcast eyes. In a kind of practical joke, Jesus got them to repeat all that had happened to this man Jesus—they had not yet recognized him—over the past few days. Then he gave them a rebuke:

> "How foolish you are, and how slow of heart to believe all that the prophets have spoken! Did not the Christ have to suffer these things and then enter his glory?" And beginning with Moses and all the Prophets, he explained to them what was said in all the Scriptures concerning himself.

Today we need an "Emmaus road" experience in reverse. The disciples knew Moses and the Prophets but could not conceive how they might relate to Jesus the Christ. The modern church knows Jesus the Christ but is fast losing any grasp of Moses and the Prophets.

Elsewhere, Jesus told a story of two men who built houses that, from the outside, looked alike. The true difference between them came to light when a storm hit. One house did not fall, even though rain poured down, streams rose, and winds beat against it, because its foundation rested on rock. The second house, foolishly built on sand, fell with a great crash. In theology as well as in construction, foundations matter.

Quick, What Is God Like?

According to Elaine Storkey, that question, "Quick, what is God like?" was asked by a five-year-old girl who rushed up to her newborn brother in his hospital room. She shrewdly figured that, having just come from Heaven, he might have some inside information. Alas, he merely made a gurgling sound and rolled his eyes.

The Old Testament provides an answer to the little girl's question, a different answer than we might get from the New Testament alone. Although Jesus is the "image of the invisible God," he emptied himself of many of the prerogatives of God in order to become a man. The late professor Langdon Gilkey used to say that if evangelical Christianity has a heresy it is the neglect of God the Father, the Creator, Preserver, and Ruler of all human history and every human community, in favor of Jesus the Son, who relates to individual souls and their destinies.

If we had only the Gospels, we would envision a God who seems confined, all-too-human, and rather weak—after all, Jesus ended up hanging on a cross. The Jews objected so strongly to Jesus because, despite his audacious claims, he did not match their conception of what God is like; they rejected him for not measuring up. The book of Revelation gives a different glimpse of Jesus—blazing light, stunning in glory, unlimited in power—and the Old Testament likewise fills in a different portrayal of God. Like Jesus' original disciples, we need that background picture in order to appreciate how much *love* the Incarnation expressed—how much God gave up on our behalf.

Apart from the Old Testament we will always have an impoverished view of God. God is not a philosophical construct but a Person who acts in history: the one who created Adam, who gave a promise to Noah, who called Abraham and introduced himself by name to Moses, who deigned to live in a wilderness *tent* in order to live close to his people. From Genesis 1 onward, God has wanted himself to be known, and the Old Testament is our most complete revelation of what God is like.

John Updike has said that "our brains are no longer conditioned for reverence and awe." The very words sound old-fashioned, and to the degree that they do, to that degree we have strayed from the picture of God revealed in the Old Testament. We cannot box him in, explain him away. God seems a wild and mysterious Other, not a God we can easily figure out. No one tells him what to do (the main point in God's blistering speech to Job).

I admit that the Old Testament introduces some problems I would rather avoid. Throughout this book I will struggle with the revelation of God I find there. "Consider therefore the kindness and sternness of God," wrote Paul to the Christians in Rome. I would rather consider only the kindness of God, but by doing so I would construct my own image of God instead of relying on God's self-revelation. I dare not speak for God without listening to God speak for himself.

It makes an enormous difference how we picture God. Is God an aloof watchmaker who winds up the universe and steps back to watch it wind down on its own? Or is God a caring parent who holds not just the universe but individual men and women in his hands? I cannot conceive of a more important project than restoring a proper notion of what God is like.

Unavoidably, we transfer to God feelings and reactions that come from our human parents. George Bernard Shaw had difficulty with God because his father had been a scoundrel, an absentee father who cared mostly about cricket and pubs. Likewise, C. S. Lewis struggled to overcome the imprint left by his own father, a harsh man who would resort to quoting Cicero to his children when scolding them. When his mother died, Lewis said, it felt as if Atlantis had broken off and left him stranded on a tiny island. After studying at a public school led by a cruel headmaster who was later certified insane and committed to an institution, Lewis had to overcome the impact of these male figures to find a way to love God.

The Old Testament portrays God as a father, yes, but a different kind of father than that encountered by Shaw and Lewis. It portrays God as a lion but also a lamb, an eagle but also a mother hen, a king but also a servant, a judge but also a shepherd. Just when we think we have God pinned down, the Old Testament introduces a whole new picture of him: as a whistler, a barber, a vineyard keeper.

Like a drumbeat that never stops, in the pages of the Old Testament we hear the consistent message that this world revolves around God, not us. The Hebrews had incessant reminders built into their culture. They dedicated their firstborn livestock and children to God, wore portions of the law on their heads and wrists, posted visible reminders on their doorways, said the word "blessed" a hundred times a day, even wore distinctive hairstyles and sewed tassels on their garments. A devout Jew could barely make it through an hour, much less an entire day, without running smack into some reminder that he or she lived in God's world. Even the Hebrew calendar marked time by events such as the Passover and Day of Atonement, not merely by the harvest cycle and the moon. The world, they believed, is God's property. And human life is "sacred," which simply means that it belongs to God to do with what he wills.

This Old Testament notion sounds very un-American. Do not our founding documents guarantee us the right to life, liberty, and the pursuit of happiness? We rebel against any interference with our personal rights, and anyone who attempts to set boundaries that might encroach on our personal space. In our secularized, industrialized environment, we can go through an entire week, not just a day, without bumping into a reminder that this is God's world.

I remember hearing a chapel message at Wheaton College during the 1970s, when the Death of God movement had reached its peak. Professor Robert Webber chose to speak on the third commandment, "Thou shalt not take the name of the Lord thy God in vain." We usually interpret that commandment in a narrow sense of prohibiting swearing, said Webber, who then proceeded to expand its meaning to "never live as though God does not exist." Or, stated positively, "Always live in awareness of God's existence." The more I study the commandment in its Old Testament environment, the more I agree with Webber. Any key to living in such awareness must be found in the great Jewish legacy of the Old Testament.

I am not proposing that we return to forelocks, phylacteries, and a diet that excludes pork and lobster. Nevertheless, I do believe we have much to learn from a people whose daily lives centered on God. When we look back on the covenant between God and the ancient Hebrews, what stands out to us is its strictness, the seeming arbitrariness of some of its laws. I see no such reaction among the Hebrews themselves. Few of them pleaded with God to loosen the dietary restrictions or eliminate some of their religious obligations. They seemed, rather, *relieved* that their God, unlike the pagan gods around them, had agreed to define a relationship with them.

As the Puritan scholar Perry Miller has said, when you have a covenant with God, you no longer have an ineffable, remote, unapproachable Deity; you have a God you can count on. The Hebrews and God had entered into a kind of story together, and everything about their lives sent back echoes of that story.

The story was a love story, from the very beginning. God chose them not because they were larger and stronger than other tribes—quite the contrary. Nor did he choose them for their moral superiority. He chose them because he loved them.

Like any starstruck lover, God yearned for a response. All the commands given the Hebrews flowed out of the very first commandment, "Love the Lord your God with all your heart and with all your soul and with all your strength." The Hebrews failed to keep that command, of course, but the reason Christians now call three-fourths of the Bible the "Old" Testament is that not even that terrible failure could cancel out God's love. God found a new way—a new covenant, or testament, of his love.

Søren Kierkegaard offers two suggestions for the reader who tackles difficult portions of the Bible. First, read it like a love letter, he says. As you struggle with language, culture, and other barriers, look on them as the necessary work to get to the main, crucial message from someone who loves you. Second, act on what you do understand. Kierkegaard dismisses the objection "There are so many obscure passages in the Holy Scriptures, whole books which are almost riddles" with the reply that he would only consider that objection from someone who had fully complied with all the passages that are easy to understand!

Is God Really Good?

For thousands of years the Jews have prayed this prayer: "Give thanks to the Lord Almighty, for the Lord is good; his love endures forever." It makes a good prayer to reflect on, because we doubt precisely those two things today. Is the Lord good? Does his love endure forever? A glance at history, or any day's headlines, and a reasonable person begins to wonder about those bold assertions. For this reason, too, the Old Testament merits our attention, because the Jews loudly doubted the very prayer they prayed. As befitting an intimate relationship, they took those doubts to the other party, to God himself, and got a direct response.

We learn from the Old Testament how God works, which is not at all as we might expect. God moves slowly, unpredictably, paradoxically. The first eleven chapters of Genesis describe a series of human failures that call the entire creation project into question. As a remedy to those failures, God declares a plan in Genesis 12: to deal with the general problem of humanity by establishing one particular family, a tribe known as the Hebrews (later called the Jews). Through them, the womb for the Incarnation, God will bring about restoration of the entire earth, back to its original design.

That plan declared, God proceeds in a most mysterious manner. To found his tribe, God chooses a pagan from the region that is now Iraq and puts him through a series of tests, many of which he fails. In Egypt, for example, Abraham demonstrates a morality inferior to that of the Sun worshipers.

After promising to bring about a people numerous as the stars in the sky and the sand on the seashore, God then proceeds to conduct a clinic in infertility. Abraham and Sarah wait into their nineties to see their first child; their daughter-in-law Rebekah proves barren for a time; her son Jacob must wait fourteen years for the wife of his dreams, only to discover her barren as well. Three straight generations of infertile women hardly seems an efficient way to populate a great nation.

After making similar promises to bring about possession of a great land (Abraham himself possessed only a grave site in Canaan), God arranges a detour for the Israelites into Egypt, where they molder for *four centuries* until Moses arrives to lead them to the Promised Land—a wretched journey that takes forty years instead of the expected two weeks. Clearly, God operates on a different timetable than that used by impatient human beings.

The surprises continue on into New Testament times, for none of the vaunted Jewish scholars recognizes Jesus of Nazareth as the Messiah trumpeted in the Psalms and Prophets. In fact, they continue today, as self-appointed prophets confidently identify a succession of tyrants and world figures as the Antichrist, only to see Hitler, Stalin, Kissinger, and Hussein fade from view.

Christians living today face many unfulfilled promises. World poverty and population continue to soar and, as a percentage of population, Christianity barely holds its own. The planet lurches toward self-destruction. We wait, and keep on waiting, for the glory days promised in the Prophets and in Revelation. From Abraham and Joseph and Moses and David we gain at least the knowledge that God moves in ways we would not predict or even desire. At times God's history seems to operate on an entirely different plane than ours.

The Old Testament gives clues into the kind of history God is writing. Exodus identifies by name the two Hebrew midwives who helped save Moses' life, but it does not bother to record the name of the Pharaoh ruling Egypt (an omission that has baffled scholars ever since). First Kings grants a total of eight verses to King Omri, even though secular historians regard him as one of Israel's most powerful kings. In his own history, God does not seem impressed by size or power or wealth. Faith is what he wants, and the heroes who emerge are heroes of faith, not strength or wealth.

God's history thus focuses on those who hold faithful to him regardless of how things turn out. When Nebuchadnezzar, one of many tyrants who persecute the Jews, threatens three young men with torture by fire, they respond:

> If we are thrown into the blazing furnace, the God we serve is able to save us from it, and he will rescue us from your hand, O king. But even if he does not, we want you to know, O king, that we will not serve your gods or worship the image of gold you have set up.

Empires rise and fall, powerful leaders soar to power, then topple from it. The same Nebuchadnezzar who tossed these three into a fiery furnace ends up demented, grazing on grass in the field like a cow. The succession of empires that follow his—Persia, Greece, Rome—so mighty in their day, join the dustbin of history even as God's people the Jews survive murderous pogroms. Slowly, painstakingly, God writes his history on earth through the deeds of his faithful followers, one by one.

Out of their tortured history, the Jews demonstrate the most surprising lesson of all: you cannot go wrong personalizing God. God is not a blurry power living somewhere in the sky, not an abstraction like the Greeks proposed, not a sensual super-human like the Romans worshiped, and definitely not the absentee watchmaker of the Deists. God is *personal.* He enters into people's lives, messes with families, shows up in unexpected places, chooses unlikely leaders, calls people to account. Most of all, God loves.

As the great Jewish theologian Abraham Heschel put it in *The Prophets,*

> To the prophet, God does not reveal himself in an abstract absoluteness, but in a personal and intimate relation to the world. He does not simply command and expect obedience; He is also moved and affected by what happens in the world, and reacts accordingly. Events and human actions arouse in him joy or sorrow, pleasure or wrath.... Man's deeds may move Him, affect Him, grieve Him or, on the other hand, gladden and please Him.
>
> ... the God of Israel is a God Who loves, a God Who is known to, and concerned with, man. He not only rules the world in the majesty of his might and wisdom, but reacts intimately to the events of history.

More than any other word pictures, God chooses "children" and "lovers" to describe our relationship with him as being intimate and personal. The Old Testament abounds with husband-bride imagery. God woos his people and dotes on them like a lover doting on his beloved. When they ignore him, he feels hurt, spurned, like a jilted lover. Shifting metaphors generationally, it also announces that we are God's children. In other words, the closest we can come to understanding how God looks upon us is by thinking about the people who mean most to us: our own child, our lover.

Think of a doting parent with a video camera, coaxing his year-old daughter to let go of the living room coffee table and take three steps toward him. "Come on, sweetie, you can do it! Just let go. Daddy's here. Come on." Think of a love-struck teenager with her phone permanently attached to her ear, reviewing every second of her day with a boy who is himself infatuated enough to be interested. Think of those two scenes and then imagine God on one end and you on the other. That is the message of the Old Testament.

The Company God Keeps

You learn a lot about a person by the friends he selects, and nothing about God proves more surprising than his choice of companions, the hand-picked objects of his intimacy. Abraham pimped for his wife, Jacob cheated his brother, Moses murdered, David murdered and committed adultery both—yet all of these ended up on God's list of favorites. Jacob got his new name *Israel* (God-struggler) after an all-night wrestling match with God, and ever since the name for God's people has harked back to that contest. God's people are, literally, the children of struggle.*

---

*Thomas F. Torrance (*The Mediation of Christ*) speculates that anti-semitism may have its origin here. Israel's conflict with God, its love-hate relationship, mirrors our own. Instead of taking out our resentment on God, however, we take it out on the Jews, God's chosen people: ". . . while our real quarrel is with the searching light of divine revelation reflected by Israel, it is against Israel itself that we vent our resentment. There we have, I believe, the root of anti-semitism. But wherever and whenever anti-semitism arises it is a clear sign that people are engaged in conflict with God and with the same kind of conflict that left its mark upon Israel. No other people has ever engaged with God in the same depth or intensity of the contradiction between man and God as Israel."

God has it out with loud complainers like Job, Jeremiah, and Jonah. He engages Abraham and Moses in lengthy arguments—and sometimes lets them win! In his wrestling match with Jacob, God waits until daybreak to inflict the wound; till then, Jacob holds his own. Quite obviously, God prefers honest disagreement to dishonest submission. He takes human beings seriously, conducts dialogues with them, includes them in his plans, listens to them.

If the Old Testament's overwhelming lesson about God is that he is personal and intimate, its overwhelming lesson about human beings is that we matter. What we say, how we behave, even what we think and feel—these things have an enormous effect on God. They have, in fact, cosmic implications.

Those of us who live in an era that has viewed our planet from the perspective of spacecraft, as a tiny globe of blue and green suspended in the unimaginable vastness of the universe, have trouble believing that we matter. Ironically, it was our most advanced technological accomplishments, such as the Hubble telescope, that exposed our cosmological tininess. Ernst Becker says that we carry in our breast "the ache of cosmic specialness," wondering how we can be an object of primary value in the universe.

Basketball bad-boy Dennis Rodman expresses the modern point of view: "If there is a supreme being, he/she/it has a hell of a lot more to worry about than my stupid problems." Actually, much of the Old Testament is devoted to overcoming that very same objection among the ancient Hebrews.

> When I consider your heavens,
>   the work of your fingers,
> the moon and the stars,
>   which you have set in place,
> what is man that you are mindful of him,
>   the son of man that you care for him?

Mesopotamian creation accounts portray human beings as almost incidental to creation, inferior beings made to serve at the whims of the gods to satisfy their personal needs. Genesis, in contrast, puts man and woman at the peak of creation and invests in them the freedom and power to determine—and spoil—all the rest. According to Cicero, "The gods attend to great matters; they neglect small ones." The Old Testament disagrees, showing instead a God who "takes delight in his people." The same Psalm 8 that begins with wonder at God's concern for humans continues:

> You made him a little lower than the heavenly beings
>   and crowned him with glory and honor.
>
> You made him ruler over the works of your hands;
>   you put everything under his feet. . . .

David and the other psalmists seem stunned by the notion that a God "high up" in the heavens could care about what happens on this puny planet, but again and again God irrefutably proves it to them. The message that our actions do matter practically defines the Old Testament. We profoundly affect God. A verse from Zephaniah in the old King James Version expresses it well:

> The Lord thy God in the midst of thee is mighty; he will save, he will rejoice over thee with joy; he will rest in his love, *he will joy over thee* with singing.

Scientists today, even agnostics, grudgingly acknowledge an "anthropic principle," for the universe is so finely tuned that it seems designed to support the existence of human life. The Old Testament pictures far more than an anthropic principle at work. God reverses the flow of all religion, which, until then, had pictured the gods as supernatural beings whose actions filter down to affect life on earth. A god cries, and it rains on earth; a god gets mad, and lightning strikes. The Old Testament shows—and nowhere more clearly than in Job—just the reverse. A desperate woman prays, and God sends a prophet; a disheartened old man refuses to curse God, and the impact reverberates throughout the cosmos.

For this reason, it can truly be said that the Jews invented history. For them, history did not simply replay cycles of eternity; human actions on earth mattered, and those very responses created history. The Sovereign Lord of history allows people to exert an influence on him, just as he exerts influence on them. Philosopher Glenn Tinder makes the distinction between Destiny and Fate. The Jews gave us all a sense of Destiny, that we exist not in a meaningless world, nor to act out some god's whim, but we exist to fulfill a meaningful Destiny ordained for us by a personal God.

Visit a museum that contains artifacts from Israel's neighbors, and you can see the shift. In Egypt or Syria you can view the gods Osiris or Lil or Astarte. A Jew can point to no such image, for graven images of God have always been forbidden. All he can do is repeat Jewish history, the story of a relationship: our God spoke to Abraham, called Moses, summoned us out of Egypt. "God," says Jack Miles, "is like a novelist who . . . can only tell his own story through his characters."

In the end, I came to love the Old Testament because it gives me a history to enter into. As I got to know the characters who sought in their various ways to "get along with God," I found myself in them. In different seasons I identified with Job, with Jacob, with the Teacher of Ecclesiastes, with the psalmists in their fluctuating moods. Through their lives with God I discovered my own.

For some time now I have been asking friends, "What is a relationship with God really like? How does it work?" Imagine the varied answers I would get to that question from Abraham, Enoch, Jeremiah, Isaiah, Moses, Jacob, David, Jonah, and Job. Each of these had radically different experiences of God, and I can enter into and learn from their encounters. Life with God is an individual matter, and general formulas do not easily apply.

Kathleen Norris tells of her experiences as a guest at a Benedictine monastery, where the monks chant the psalms daily, proceeding through all 150 psalms in a month. At first Norris felt confused and jarred by the dissonance of the psalms, some of which express pious comfort while others cry out against God's absence or unfairness. Over time, though, as she got to know the monks and other guests who chanted the psalms, she realized that *someone* in the cloister was identifying with the words of each psalm. Each one reflected some facet of life with God, and those with eyes to see and ears to hear perceived the needed message.

Contemporary Christianity, with its narrow focus on the Epistles, has, for me, neglected this truth. Growing up in evangelical churches, I got my pictures of the Christian life exclusively from Paul who, I would suggest, is hardly a "typical" Christian. Paul had a miraculous conversion experience, had a history of miracles and supernatural interventions, and—apart from Romans 7, bless that chapter—apparently had an easy time living out the lofty ideals of the Christian life, or at least an easier time than I have. Once Paul understood something intellectually, his emotions tended to line up in good order. Trying to imitate Paul (which he encouraged) is, in my experience, no simpler than trying to imitate Jesus.

In the Old Testament I discovered a rich tapestry of encounters with God that added an important background to Paul's example. In the Psalms, for example, I found disorientation, confusion, rage, despair, and anguish such that I had never heard discussed in my church. We were too quick to move on to a "higher" experience of spiritual victory. Astonishingly, I learned that these "problematic" psalms were the ones the New Testament—and especially Jesus—quoted most often!

I have long struggled with the impossible ideals of the Sermon on the Mount and the self-assured, God-said-it-so-do-it tone of the Epistles. I found a remarkably different approach in books like Proverbs and Ecclesiastes. They use a moderate, "Golden Mean" approach: make money but not too much; have fun without getting hedonistic. These are, in fact, the principles parents have always used in training children; I cannot imagine rearing a three-year-old on the principles of the Sermon on the Mount.

I do not mean to draw a sharp distinction between the New Testament and the Old. Quite the contrary. It would be a mistake to read the Old Testament merely to contrast it with the New or to add to our understanding of the New. It has a reality in itself. The Old Testament is not, as one theologian suggested, "reading someone else's mail"; it is our mail as well. The people who appear in it were real people learning to get along with the same God that I worship. I need to learn from their experience even as I try to incorporate the marvelous new message brought by Jesus and developed by Paul and the others.

Spiritual Journal

As I was in the process of writing this very chapter, a sad event occurred: my father-in-law died. Hunter Norwood lived a rich, full life of eighty years. He sailed to South America as a missionary in 1942, built a house in the jungle by hand, founded a church and Bible Institute, and later returned to the U.S. to direct a mission organization. Along the way he and his wife raised six wonderful daughters, one of whom I married.

Hunter was a Bible teacher *par excellence,* and even after retirement he sought out ways to teach the Bible. He taught extension courses for Moody Bible Institute. He drove forty-five minutes each Sunday to teach the Bible to a Presbyterian church class. When his health began failing, he would sit in front of the class in a wheelchair, speaking into a microphone in a bare whisper. A few years ago I hired him to help with some revisions of *The Student Bible* because I knew no one I could better trust with biblical research.

Eventually, due to cancer and a nerve-degenerating disease, the time came when Hunter Norwood could no longer teach the Bible. He still studied it faithfully each day and prayed through a list of all the people he had ministered to over the years. He believed wholeheartedly in the Victorious Christian Life and named Romans as his favorite book, his guidebook on relating to God. As illness progressed, however, he began questioning some aspects of the Victorious Christian Life. Little wonder, in view of his condition. He had a catheter installed. He lost control of his bowels. His gums shriveled so that he could hardly keep dentures in, and visitors kept asking him to repeat what he had said. His hands trembled, and he often dropped things. It is hard to maintain a spirit of joy and victory when your body rebels against you, when you must call for help to drink a glass of water or blow your nose.

During the last two years of his life, Hunter's world shrank to the size of a single bedroom, then to the size of a hospital bed, which he rarely left. There, up until the day he could no longer hold a pen, he recorded his journal of wrestling with God. I am holding that journal, a spiral-bound notebook, on my lap as I write. Starting from the back, I find lists of the people he prayed for faithfully, seventeen pages of lists: his extended family (there is my own name, beside my wife's), the Indians in South America, the students in his many Bible classes, the missionaries he used to lead, his church, widows, his neighbors. Stains—coffee, food, tears—mark the pages.

If I flip the notebook and start from the other side, I find Hunter Norwood's journal of relating to God. It goes on for nineteen pages, and I can watch the progression of his disease in the handwriting that deteriorates on each page. Mostly, he quotes a Bible verse or briefly comments on it. A few times he writes about his physical condition: sore back, legs not working, losing strength, dehydrated. The last entry, barely legible, is marked August 7, almost exactly one year before he died. Throughout that final year, he could not write.

What strikes me about the journal is this: of the hundreds of entries, I can find only nine referring to verses in the New Testament. I see entries like this:

Psalm 28. Father help! I feel low, sad, fearful.

2 Kings 11–14. So few seem faithful to God, but He has compassion and mercy!

Psalm 53:5. There they were overwhelmed with dread when there was nothing to dread.

Psalm 59:4. Arise to help me, look on my plight.

Job 42:2. I know You can do all things. No plan of Yours can be thwarted!

Psalm 71:14. But as for me, I will always have hope!

Psalm 20:1. May the Lord answer you when you are in distress, and may the Lord protect you!

2 Chronicles 28:20. Do not be *afraid* or *discouraged* for the Lord my God is with you.

Lamentations 3:26. It is good to wait quietly for the salvation of the Lord.

Psalm 139. Fearfully and wonderfully made.

Psalm 27. The Lord is the stronghold of my life, of whom shall I be afraid?

Job 23:10. When He has tested me I will come forth as gold.

Psalm 40:17. O my God do not delay!

Job 36:15. He speaks to them in their affliction.

Jeremiah 46:28. Do not fear, O Jacob, my servant, for I am with you, declares the Lord.

Psalm 116:15. Precious in the sight of the Lord is the death of His saints.

Psalm 121:2. My *help* comes from the *Lord.*
Psalm 10:14. But You, O God, *do see trouble and grief.*

Those of us who knew Hunter Norwood well know that the last few years of his life were by far the hardest. Opponents of his faith had stoned him in Colombia. He coped with alligators, boa constrictors, and piranhas in Peru. He brought up six daughters in two different cultures. But none of these compared to the difficulties of lying in bed all day, his body defying his every command, waiting to die. Toward the end, it took all his effort to accomplish the simple acts of swallowing and breathing.

Hunter went through a crisis of faith in those last few years, which he talked about openly. Answers that used to satisfy him no longer did. He lost spiritual confidence, not in God but in himself. As he grew anxious, impatient, and fearful, he wept bitter tears over his own inability to maintain composure. In the face of death, he longed to "finish well," a phrase he kept using. Yet again and again he disappointed himself. He feared disappointing God.

The wavering yet rock-solid faith Hunter found in the Old Testament sustained him when nothing else could. Even at his most doubt-filled moments, he took comfort in the fact that some of God's favorites had battled the very same demons. He learned that the arms of the Lord are long and wrap around those he loves, not just in prosperous and happy times but especially in times of travail. I am glad that, in those dark days, Hunter Norwood had the Old Testament to fall back on.

TWO

Job:
Seeing in the Dark

TWO

Job: Seeing in the Dark

Is it worth the lion's while to terrify the mouse?

—CARL JUNG

Because I began my career as a magazine journalist telling other people's stories, early in my twenties I ran smack into the problem of suffering. While tracking down various article leads, I would find myself by the bed of someone blindsided by tragedy. A teenager mauled by a grizzly bear as he tried to rescue his girlfriend, a father who died while sheltering his children with his body during a blizzard on Mount Rainier, a man who lived out a life of crime in angry rebellion against the abuse he had suffered in childhood—I wrote these and other stories for the *Reader's Digest* "Drama in Real Life" series.

Every single person I interviewed told me that the tragedy they had undergone pushed them to the wall with God. Sadly, each person also gave a devastating indictment of the church: Christians, they said, made matters worse. One by one, Christians visited their hospital rooms with pet theories: God is punishing you; No, not God, it's Satan!; No, it's God, who hand-picked you to give him glory; It's neither God nor Satan, you just happened to get in the way of an angry mother bear.

As one survivor told me, "The theories about pain confused me, and none of them helped. Mainly, I wanted assurance and comfort, from God and from God's people. In almost every case the Christians brought more pain and little comfort."

I wrote *Where Is God When It Hurts* in direct response to this problem. The pain of those I interviewed had become my pain; their questions became my questions. Later, in response to hundreds of letters that raised many more issues about God and suffering, I wrote a kind of sequel, *Disappointment with God.* Although my writing has since moved on to other topics, I have never stopped thinking about the questions that haunted me in my earlier years as a journalist.

The problem of pain is not one you can neatly solve, then file away. It roars to life every time a tornado touches down, every time a neighbor learns bad news about a disabled child, every time someone in my family hears the ugly diagnosis of cancer, every time a physical symptom forces me to the doctor. We are born slathered in blood and bodily fluids, amid tears and cries of pain; we die in like manner; and in between birth and death we ask, *Why?*

For this reason I find myself returning again and again to the book of Job, the Bible's fullest treatment of the problem of suffering. That, at least, is what I used to think. If you had asked me a decade ago what the book of Job was about, I would have replied without hesitation: *Job? Everybody knows what Job is about. It's the Bible's most comprehensive look at the problem of pain and suffering.*

I still refer to Job whenever I write about suffering, and without doubt the bulk of the book (chapters 3–37) revolves around the theme. Those chapters render no action to speak of, just five prickly men—Job, his three friends, and the mostly silent Elihu—sitting around discussing theories about pain. Much like the hospital visitors described by my interview subjects, Job's friends were trying to account for the "slings and arrows of outrageous fortune" that fell upon poor Job. They achieved about the same result as the hospital visitors, making Job even more miserable.

In the Old Testament, faithful believers such as Job and his friends acted shocked when suffering came their way, for they quite reasonably expected God to reward them with prosperity and health. The book of Job represents a step beyond the "contract faith" assumed in most of the Old Testament: Do good and get blessed, do bad and get punished. Indeed, many scholars believe the book of Job crucially helped Israel come to terms with the series of calamities that crashed down upon the nation. This classic story of one person gave voice to questions that plagued the entire nation: How can God's "chosen people" suffer so many disasters?

Job does in fact focus on the problem of suffering, but in a most unexpected way. It brilliantly asks the questions we most urgently want answered, then turns aside to propose another way of looking at the problem entirely. Like most of the Old Testament, Job at first frustrates, by refusing the simple answers we think we want, and then oddly satisfies, by pointing us in a new direction marked by flagrant realism and a tantalizing glimpse of hope.

A Timeless Story

The book of Job so fascinated John Calvin that 159 of his 700 sermons centered on it. History since Calvin has only increased the urgency of these issues, and we moderns cannot get enough of Job's story. Its motif of undeserved suffering seems peculiarly suited to our own pain-wracked century, an era that has included two world wars, two atom bomb attacks, and more than its share of genocide campaigns. As a result, the portrait of genial old Job, moaning mournfully while life caves in around him, seems to fit a favorite modern stereotype.

Neil Simon borrowed the Job setting for a play, *God's Favorite*, as did Archibald MacLeish (*J.B.*) and Robert Frost (*The Masque of Reason*). More recently, novelist Muriel Spark updated the plot of Job in a modern setting (*The Only Problem*). Even the play *Amadeus* owes much of its plot twist to Job, for its playwright put a reverse spin on the very same issue. Job wondered why he, an innocent man, was suffering God's judgment; the composer Salieri questioned how Mozart, a genius-brat, had earned divine favor.

All the recent take-offs explore the conundrum posed by the original Old Testament book. Job's friends insisted that a just, loving, and powerful God ought to follow certain rules on earth, mainly by rewarding those who do good and punishing those who do evil. Virtually every statement by those loquacious friends reduces down to this basic contention: since Job was suffering, he must have sinned.

For Job, who knew his own soul, the facts did not add up. He had done nothing to deserve such an outbreak of calamities. And for us too the facts do not add up. We see the face of unexplained suffering wherever we look: Jews in the Holocaust, famine victims in Africa, Christians in Moslem prisons. Those who still subscribe to the neat formula of Job's friends—and there are many, if religious broadcasts give any indication—would do well to consider one sobering fact: the most aggressively Christian continent on earth, Africa, is also the hungriest, while the most aggressively non-Christian region, around the Arabian Sea, is the wealthiest. (When Robert Schuller compiled *The Possibility Thinker's Bible*, he found only fourteen verses to highlight in the book of Job.)

In truth, the questions asked so eloquently by Job have not faded away over the centuries, but have grown even louder and shriller. Spark's novel *The Only Problem* gets its title from a phrase in a conversation about how a good God can allow suffering. "It's the only problem, in fact, worth discussing," concludes her protagonist. The problem of pain is a modern obsession, the theological kryptonite of our time, and the ancient man Job expressed it as well as it has ever been expressed.

Yet despite all the echoes in modern literature, despite my own reliance on Job as I write about pain, despite the fact that all but a few pages of Job focus on the problem of pain, I have concluded that Job is not about the problem of pain at all. Details of suffering serve as the ingredients of the story, the stuff of which it is made, not the central theme.

A cake is not "about" eggs, flour, milk and shortening; a chef merely uses those ingredients in the process of creating a cake. In the same way, Job is not "about" the vagaries of suffering but merely uses those ingredients in its author's overall scheme. Seen as a whole, the book of Job is about faith, the story of one man selected to undergo a staggering ordeal by trial. His response presents a message that applies not just to suffering people, but to every person who lives on planet Earth.

Chapters 3–37 of Job, which center on the issue of suffering, are preceded by the "plot" of the book as reported in chapters 1–2, and that plot affects the context of everything that follows. Most of the time, our visual faculties admit a narrow spectrum of "natural" light; we have no certain knowledge of what might be going on behind the scenes. Job temporarily lifts our blinders. Somewhat like Elisha's servant, who suddenly saw the "chariots of fire" that had been surrounding him, we gain through this book a glimpse of supernatural activity normally hidden from view.

It helps to think of Job as a mystery play, a "whodunit" detective story. We in the audience have showed up early for a press conference in which the director explains his work (chapters 1–2). We learn in advance who did what in the play, and we understand that the personal drama on earth has its origin in a cosmic drama in heaven—the contest over Job's faith. Will Job believe in God or deny God?

The author of Job is a born playwright: dispensing with the action in two chapters, he gravitates quickly to his more natural form of dialogue. The curtains lower, and when they go up again we see only the actors on stage who, confined within the play, have no knowledge of the omniscient point of view enjoyed by us in the audience. Although we know the answer to the "whodunit" questions, the star detective does not. From the outset Job, unaware of the scenario that went on in the heavens, is trapped in the ingredients of the drama. Obsessed with suffering, he spends his time on stage trying to discover what we viewers already know. He scratches himself with shards of pottery and asks trenchant questions, the same questions asked by nearly everyone in great pain. Why me? What did I do wrong? What is God trying to tell me?

For the audience, Job's whodunit questions should be moot, for we already know the answers. What has Job done wrong? Nothing. God himself called Job "blameless and upright, a man who fears God and shuns evil" (2:3). Why is Job suffering? We know in advance that he is not being punished. Far from it, he has been selected as the principal subject in a great contest of the heavens. Job represents the very best of the species, and God is using him to prove to Satan that a human being's faith can be genuine and selfless, not dependent on God's good gifts. Such a cosmic contest poses its own problems, of course, but these are different problems than most people grapple with when unexpected suffering hits.

By allowing us the glimpse behind the curtain in chapters 1 and 2, the author of Job forfeits all elements of narrative tension but one: the mystery of how Job will respond. In short, only the question of his faith remains unanswered. It is a testament to the genius of the book, and a clue as to why it endures as a work of literature, that we can forget chapters 1 and 2 and get swept up in Job's personal anguish. He struggles with the imponderables of suffering with such force that, for the duration of the book, his questions become our questions.

In his speeches Job marshals every example of unfairness in the world that he can find. Those of us who know the full story, especially the ending, can miss the impact of those words of anguish. One does not expect to discover the arguments of God's greatest adversaries—say, Mark Twain's *Letters from the Earth* or Bertrand Russell's *Why I Am Not a Christian*—bound into the center of the Bible. Such, however, is characteristic of the Old Testament. As William Safire put it, "The Book of Job delights the irreverent, satisfies the blasphemous, and offers at least some comfort to the heretical."

The Contest

Many readers move quickly from the befuddling scene in chapters 1–2 to the friends' lofty discourses, God's grand nature poetry, and the few—shockingly few, for all the attention they receive—rays of hope in Job's speeches. Yet behind all that follows, we must constantly remind ourselves, looms the background setting of those first two chapters. The director has explained in advance the nature of the contest.

Some commentators treat chapters 1 and 2 with a tone of mild embarrassment, giving the distinct impression they would prefer it if Job began with chapter 3. Novelist Virginia Woolf wrote a friend, "I read the book of Job last night—I don't think God comes well out of it." The prologue shows God and Satan involved in—and you can almost see blush marks on the commentary pages—well, something resembling a wager. The two have a kind of bet going, in which God has stacked the odds against himself. Poor Job must undergo a terrible ordeal in order to determine the winner between the two heavyweights. In a sense, Job must replay the original test of the garden of Eden, with the bar raised higher. Living in paradise, Adam and Eve faced a best-case scenario for trusting God, who asked so little of them and showered down blessings. In a living hell, Job faces the worst-case scenario: God asks so much, while curses rain down on him.

The contest posed between Satan and God is no trivial exercise. Satan's accusation that Job loves God only because "you have put a hedge around him," stands as an attack on God's character. It implies that God is not worthy of love in himself, that people follow God only because they get something out of it or are "bribed" to do so. In Satan's view, God resembles a politician who can win only by rigging the election, or a mafioso with a "kept woman" and not a devoted wife. People love God, said one priest, "the way a peasant loves his cow, for the butter and cheese it produces." Job's response, after all the props of faith have been removed, will prove or disprove Satan's challenge. A wealthy man, Job has much to lose if God stops blessing him. Will he continue to trust God even after he forfeits it all?

The book hinges on the issue of integrity. Job acts as if God's integrity is on trial: How can a loving God treat him so unjustly? All of Job's legal briefs, however, surface within the setting of the larger trial set up in chapters 1–2, the test of Job's faith. God seeks, as a line from Handel tells it, "love unsought by price or fear." From our omniscient readers' viewpoint, we watch for cracks in Job's own integrity as he loses, one by one, everything he values.

The story of Job strikes a sympathetic chord with us moderns because we too have put God on trial over the issue of suffering. Eloquently, powerfully, we demand answers from God, and God's treatment of Job is one of those issues we shake our heads over. We retell Job's story, quote him, take comfort in his words of protest. Job gives voice to some of our most deeply felt complaints. "We cry into the night and there is no reply," said Bertrand Russell.

That we find such sympathy for Job's predicament reveals much about our modern attitude toward God. Significantly, all the modern retellings of the ancient story cast Job as a tragically heroic figure. Elie Wiesel goes so far as to scold Job for giving in to God. After surviving the Holocaust, Wiesel has no sympathy for a character who would surrender to God so abjectly. He prefers to believe that the true ending of the book was lost, and that "Job died without having humiliated himself; that he succumbed to his grief an uncompromising and whole man."

C. S. Lewis put his finger on the reason behind our empathetic response in his essay "God in the Dock":

> The ancient man approached God (or even the gods) as the accused person approaches his judge. For the modern man the roles are reversed. He is the judge: God is in the dock. He is quite a kindly judge: if God should have a reasonable defence for being the god who permits war, poverty and disease, he is ready to listen to it. The trial may even end in God's acquittal. But the important thing is that Man is on the Bench and God in the Dock.

Although Job may help us form our questions about unjust suffering, it fails to give many answers for a very simple reason: chapters 1–2 have clearly shown that, regardless of what Job thinks, God is not on trial in this book. Job is on trial. The book does not provide answers to the problem of pain— "Where is God when it hurts?"—for the prologue has already dispensed with that issue. The point is faith: Where is Job? How is he responding?

The more I studied Job, the more I realized I had always read the book from the perspective of chapter 3 on. I needed to go back and reconsider the message of Job from the very first chapter. There, I located the core plot: the best man on earth suffers the worst calamities, which poses a test of faith in its most extreme form.

Are human beings truly free? Satan challenged God on that count. We have freedom to descend, of course—Satan himself, Adam, and everyone who has ever lived has proved that. But do we have the freedom and ability to ascend, to believe God for no other reason than, well ... for no reason at all? Can a person believe even when God appears to him as an enemy? Or is faith, like everything else, a product of environment and circumstances?

The modern behaviorist Edward O. Wilson explains Mother Teresa's good deeds by pointing out she was secure in the service of Christ and in her belief in immortality; in other words, believing she would get her reward she acted on that "selfish" basis. There is no pure altruism, say Wilson and other evolutionary psychologists. We have faith in God in hopes that we will get something out of it.

In the opening chapters of Job, Satan reveals himself as the first great behaviorist. Job is conditioned to love God, he claims. Take away the positive rewards, and watch faith crumble. Job, oblivious and effectively blindfolded, ranks as the main protagonist in a single-warrior combat test of the ages.

Job's Friends

Satan does not make an appearance after chapter 2 of Job, nor does he need to, since Job's friends ably represent his point of view. In a splendid stroke of dramatic irony, most of the book's high-sounding (but false) theology comes from the mouths of pious, devout men, who, at the end, get leveled by a withering blast from God.

Job's three friends, and to a lesser extent Elihu, follow the behaviorist party line. Common sense and all reason tell us, they argue, that a just God will treat people fairly. Those who obey and remain faithful, God rewards. Those who sin, God punishes. Who could refute that? They then take the next logical step of concluding that Job's extreme suffering must betray some serious, unconfessed sin. If Job only stopped being so stubborn and repented, God would surely pardon and restore him.

Job's friends get bad press, and rightly so since God summarily dismisses them in the end. Nonetheless, they are not men of straw. They argue forcefully, and their calm reasoning contrasts with Job's uncontrolled outbursts. I would suggest that if today we had only Job 3–37, we would judge the three friends as the true heroes of the book. Why do I say that? Simply because their arguments are still being sounded in Christian churches.

To truly grasp the prescience and timelessness of the book, consider the arguments of Bildad, Eliphaz, and Zophar in light of contemporary thinking. Does God send suffering as punishment for sins? Ask any hospitalized Christian whether he or she has heard that suggestion. The most vigorous assertion of Job's friends—that God makes good men prosper and evil men stumble—I hear virtually every time I watch religious television. Those programs say little about Job's kind of faith, which perseveres even when nothing works out the way it should. Christians today may also claim a "word of knowledge" to back up their beliefs, as did Eliphaz. He appeals to a cryptic vision of a "spirit" who restates Eliphaz's own line of argument and even implies that Job should turn to God for a miracle (4:12–17, 5:8–10).

In short, Job's friends emerge as self-righteous dogmatists who defend the mysterious ways of God. Confident of their proper doctrine and sound arguments, they cast judgment on Job. To them the issue seems clear-cut: given a choice between a man who claims to be just and a God they know to be just, what possible defense could Job have? George MacDonald compares their attitude to that of the Pharisees, who care more about paying court to God and following the rules than coming into God's presence as children. Job, like any wounded child, insisted on his right to demand some explanation.

True to their piety, Job's friends are scandalized by his outbursts. The very idea of his questioning God, even demanding an audience with the Almighty! A modern-day bumper sticker succinctly captures their condescending tone: "If you feel far from God, guess who moved."

Job

Trapped in the "ingredients" of the drama, Job concerns himself exclusively with the issue of suffering. Of course, he knows nothing about the cosmic contest of faith—being privy to such inside information would keep his trial from being fair. Thus he feels betrayed by God.

Job faces an impossible dilemma. To reject God would shatter his bedrock faith in a loving God, the most important value in his life. However, to admit that suffering is deserved would also compromise his integrity, for he believes himself innocent of anything that might merit such an extreme penalty. His friends describe a terrible battle between good and evil; Job is fighting an even more terrible moral battle, between good and good. God's justice has collided head-on with Job's innocence. Nothing makes sense any more.

In the face of his friends' verbal assaults, Job wavers, contradicts himself, and sometimes even agrees with them. He has no theological refutations and acknowledges that what they say sounds true. Yet in his particular case, he believes deeply that they are wrong, that he does not deserve his fate. He has sinned, yes, but not in a way to "deserve" such punishment from God, losing his family, his health, and all his possessions in short order. Toward the end of the book, Job lays out a formal legal defense of his relative innocence.

Job's speeches contain profound expressions of pain, despair, and outrage. Barely able to restrain the satire, he vents angry protests against God, wandering just to the edge of blasphemy. The first words he gets out of his mouth are these: "May the day of my birth perish, and the night it was said, 'A boy is born!'"

Listen to a sampling of quotations from this "patient" saint:

[To God] Will you never look away from me,
   or let me alone even for an instant? (7:19)

Turn away from me so I can have a moment's joy
before I go to the place of no return. (10:20–21)

But as a mountain erodes and crumbles
    and as a rock is moved from its place,
as water wears away stones
    and torrents wash away the soil,
        so you destroy man's hope. (14:18–19)

God assails me and tears me in his anger
    and gnashes his teeth at me. (16:9)

Though I cry, "I've been wronged!" I get no response;
    though I call for help, there is no justice. (19:7)

I cry out to you, O God, but you do not answer;
    I stand up, but you merely look at me.
You turn on me ruthlessly;
    with the might of your hand you attack me. . . .
Yet when I hoped for good, evil came;
    when I looked for light, then came darkness.
The churning inside me never stops. (30:20–21, 26–7)

To Job in his misery, God seems a villain who "destroys both the blameless and the wicked" (9:22)—the reverse image of Jesus' concept of a merciful Father whose sun shines on the righteous and unrighteous. As C. S. Lewis said in his journal of grief after his wife's death, "Not that I am (I think) in much danger of ceasing to believe in God. The real danger is of coming to believe such dreadful things about Him. The conclusion I dread is not 'So there's no God after all,' but 'So this is what God's really like. Deceive yourself no longer.'" Is God a Cosmic Sadist? asked Lewis with characteristic bluntness, echoing Job's doubts.

None of Job's near-blasphemies slip past his friends. Eliphaz indignantly retorts, "But you even undermine piety and hinder devotion to God" (15:4). He likens Job to a wicked man who "shakes his fist at God and vaunts himself against the Almighty" (15:25).

Yet the tale of Job has an ironic twist. As Søren Kierkegaard put it, "The secret in Job, the vital force, the nerve, the idea, is that Job, despite everything, is in the right."

A Slim Victory

In spite of Job's state of high dudgeon, he ultimately triumphs. God concludes, "I am angry with you [Eliphaz] and your two friends, because you have not spoken of me what is right, as my servant Job has." In view of Job's fierce words, how could God honor him over his friends? To put it crudely, how does God "win the wager" over Job's faith?

First, in an overall sense, Job never does follow his wife's advice to "Curse God and die." He questions God's fairness and goodness and love, and despairs of his own life, yet he refuses to turn his back on God. "Though he slay me, yet will I hope in him," he defiantly insists (13:15). Job may have given up on God's justice, but he steadfastly refuses to give up on God. At the most unlikely moments of despair, he comes up with brilliant flashes of hope and faith.

Job prefers to live with an agonizing paradox, that God still loves him even though all evidence points against it. His friends laid out the logic: *Suffering comes from God. God is just. Therefore you, Job, are guilty.* After examining his own life, and toying with the notion of an unjust God, Job arrives at a different formula that on the surface makes no sense: *Suffering comes from God. God is just. I am innocent.* In the best Hebrew tradition, Job clings to all three of those truths no matter how contradictory they seem.

Job instinctively believes he is better off casting his lot with God, regardless of how remote or even sadistic God appears at the moment, rather than abandoning all hope. He keeps alive a vision of a personal universe. In an impersonal universe, by what standard could we judge pain worse than pleasure or Job's happy life superior to his tragic life? Job holds tight to a belief in justice and a personal God in spite of the mountainous evidence against that belief, because to him the alternatives look far worse.

In addition, what Job asks from God reveals much about his character. (I know what I would have demanded: Take away the sores, God! First restore my health and then we can discuss what lesson I should learn from these disasters.) Job has other requests. As despair sinks down on him, and he feels his own faith leaking away, he asks for a quick death. Why? "Then I would still have this consolation—my joy in unrelenting pain—that I had not denied the words of the Holy One" (6:10).

When death does not come, and Job senses his prayers to be hopeless cries hurled into the void, he asks for a mediator, or arbitrator, "to lay his hand upon us both." His pleas (9:33, 16:19–21) will later find poignant fulfillment as prophecies of Jesus, the mediator between God and man, but Job himself receives no answer at the time. He has no arbitrator.

Finally, in desperation, Job reduces his demands to one request, which he sticks to until the end. He asks for a personal explanation from God himself (13:3, 31:35). He wants a day in court, a chance to hear God testify on his own behalf against what looms as a gross injustice.

This last request arouses Job's friends to fury. What right has he, an insignificant human being, to call God into account? How could a "man, who is but a maggot—a son of man, who is only a worm" (25:6) oppose the God of the universe? As Mark Twain cynically calculated, "I could as easily injure a planet by throwing mud at it." Job will not back down. To the end, he insists on his right to question God, to demand an explanation. That request, God honors.

Viktor Frankl, survivor of a Nazi concentration camp, concluded that the worst despair is suffering without meaning, and Job's experience bears that out. He demands an explanation of his trauma, a meaning to his suffering, and only God can provide that answer.

Job ultimately passes the test of faith by clinging to belief in God even though he has no evidence in support of that belief and much against it. And he insists on his own human dignity even as it is being assailed on all sides. One might call Job the first Protestant, in the fullest sense of the word. He takes his stand upon individual faith rather than yielding to pious dogma, thus paving the way for others to follow: the apostle Paul taking on the Sanhedrin, Martin Luther standing against the full authority of the church. Job refuses to let dogma overwhelm his personal rights.

William Safire summarized the legacy of Job in his book *The First Dissident*:

> If the Book of Job reaches across two and a half millennia to teach anything to men and women who consider themselves normal, decent human beings, it is this: Human beings are sure to wander in ignorance and to fall into error, and it is better—more righteous in the eyes of God—for them to react by questioning rather than accepting. Confronted with inexplicable injustice, it is better to be irate than resigned.

Safire says about Job, "I started my journey into this book with doubt in my faith and have come out with faith in my doubt."

God Appears

Ironically, God enters the scene in a swirling, disruptive storm just as Elihu is explaining why puny Job has no right to ask for divine intervention. I like to envision this scene as a kind of cartoon: two tiny figures are arguing passionately about what God will and won't do just as a massive thunderhead—God himself—races across the horizon to engulf them. God stuns everyone, both by showing up and by what he says.

God's magnificent speech in Job 38–42 has attracted much attention, especially from environmentalists who cite it as an example of the Creator's pride in the natural world. I too marvel at the wonderful images from nature—ostriches, mountain sheep, wild donkeys, crocodiles—and yet along with my marvel comes a nagging sense of bewilderment. God's speech seems most striking in what it does *not* say. In fact, the speech avoids the issue of suffering entirely, astonishing after 35 chapters full of nothing else. Why does God sidestep the very questions that have been tormenting poor Job?

God's choice of content leads back to chapters 1–2, the origin of Job's drama as seen "behind the curtain." Job and his friends have been discussing suffering because, trapped in the "ingredients" of the drama, they can see nothing else. God, of course, has known all along that the real question traces back to the original challenge of Job's faith. Will a human being trust a sovereign, invisible God even when everything around him confutes that trust?

God does not enlighten Job on the cosmic struggle he has unwittingly been involved in, because letting Job see behind the curtain would change the rules of the contest still being determined. Nor does God show the slightest bit of sympathy for Job's physical or emotional condition. To the contrary, God turns the tables on Job, rushing in fiercely,

> Who is this that darkens my counsel
>   with words without knowledge?
> Brace yourself like a man;
>   I will question you,
>   and you shall answer me, (38:2–3)

and proceeding from there to sweep Job off his feet. In other words, God abruptly puts Job back in the dock.

God's message, expressed in gorgeous poetry, boils down to something like this: Until you know a little more about running the physical universe, Job, don't tell me how to run the moral

61

universe. By describing the wonders of nature, relishing especially its wildness, God hints at some of the inherent limitations
of natural law and of his preference not to intervene. God criti-
cizes Job for only one thing, his limited point of view. Job has
based his judgments on incomplete evidence—an insight that
those of us in the "audience" have seen all along. To correct that
misconception, God expands Job's range of vision from his own
miserable circumstances to the entire universe.

I have a hunch that God could have read a page from the
phone book and Job would have meekly consented. His doubts
melt before a revelation of the power and glory of God. "Surely
I spoke of things I did not understand, things too wonderful for
me to know" (42:3), Job says. And with that repentance, and rec-
onciliation with God, the tension from chapter 1 finally resolves.

The contest has dealt with Job's faith: Will a man cling to
faith when every self-interested reason for doing so is yanked
away? "He will curse you to your face," Satan gambled. And he
loses. Job's character holds up.

His lecture delivered, God lavishes rewards on Job, making
him twice as prosperous as he was before—a resolution that
even fits Job's friends' flawed idea of God's justice. Pain? God
can fix that easily. More camels and oxen? No problem. Some
people like to dwell on the good-news account of Job's restored
fortunes, emphasizing that Job underwent trials only for a season before receiving compensation. The overall thrust of the
book, however, convinces me that faith, not rewards, is the
book's main emphasis. I say this carefully, but from God's viewpoint Job's material prosperity and even his health paled in significance when compared to the cosmic issues involved.

Job-like Times

Because of the unique angle of vision afforded in chapters 1–2,
the saga of Job illuminates far more than the exaggerated trials

of a sad old man. I began this chapter by saying I once thought I knew what Job was about: the problem of suffering. Now I realize that what many readers do to the book of Job is a paradigm of what we do to life in general. We take a story about a battleground of faith and testing and turn it into a story about suffering.

At root, Job faced a crisis of faith, not of suffering. And so do we. All of us at times find ourselves in a Job-like state. We may not face the extreme disasters that befell Job, but a tragic accident, a terminal illness, or the loss of a job may have us shaking our heads and asking, "Why me? What does God have against me? Why does God seem so distant?"

At such times we focus too easily on circumstances—illness, our looks, poverty, bad luck—as the enemy. We pray for God to change those circumstances. If only I were beautiful or handsome, we think, then everything would work out. If only I had more money, or at least a good job; if only my sexual desires would somehow change, or at least diminish—then I could easily believe God. Job teaches, though, that we need faith most at the precise moment when it seems impossible.

When tragedy strikes, we too will be trapped in a limited point of view. Like Job, we will be tempted to blame God and see him as the enemy. Job asked God poignantly, "Does it please you to oppress me, to spurn the work of your hands?" (10:3). The view behind the curtain in chapters 1–2 reveals that Job was being exalted, not spurned. God was letting his own reputation ride on the response of a single human being. At the time when Job felt most abandoned, at that very time God was giving him personal, almost microscopic scrutiny. God seemed absent; in one sense God had never been more present.

I hesitate to write this because it is a hard truth, one I do not want to acknowledge: Job convinces me that God cares more about our faith than our pleasure. That statement does not fit with the cloying, teddy-bear image of God often presented by

Christians. I may not arrive at such a conclusion if Job stood alone, but think back to the trials some of God's favorite people have undergone.

In a message to Ezekiel (14:14) God includes Job in a list of three giants of righteousness. The other two mentioned, Noah and Daniel, learned faith in the midst of a massive flood and a den of lions. Abraham had a test of faith surely as severe as Job's: he was called upon (he thought at the time) to commit the tragedy himself by sacrificing the son he had awaited many decades. David? One need only read Psalm 22 to learn of his experience with the silence of God. A comment from Deuteronomy about the Israelites in the wilderness defines the biblical pattern: "Remember how the Lord your God led you all the way in the desert these forty years, to humble you and to test you in order to know what was in your heart" (8:2).

Søren Kierkegaard, who lived a Job-like existence of inner torment, ultimately concluded that the purest faith, refined as gold, emerges from just such a state of paradox, or suspension of what we might expect from God. He kept the book of Job in bed with him at night, like a child who puts his schoolbook under his pillow to make sure he has not forgotten his lesson when he wakes up in the morning. To him, people like Job and Abraham shone as Knights of Faith. Through their harrowing ordeals of faith, they achieved a level of fidelity obtainable in no other way. Said Kierkegaard, "With the help of the thorn in my foot, I spring higher than anyone with sound feet."

Even the Son of God on earth felt a sense of being abandoned by God. Like the Israelites in the wilderness, Jesus went through a trial by ordeal to "know what was in his heart." Later, in a far more severe trial, Jesus cried out on the cross (quoting Psalm 22), "My God, why have you forsaken me?" Like Job, he continued to trust God despite the God-forsaken feeling: "Into thy hands I commit my spirit." For him too, at the very moment when God seemed most absent, at that moment the Father had never been more present. Paul tells us that on the cross God was "in Christ . . . reconciling the world to himself."

Cosmic Matters

Why does God permit, even encourage such tests of faith? Could it possibly matter to God whether one man or one woman accepts or rejects him? Elihu, the last and most mysterious of Job's comforters, scorned the very notion of God caring about Job's predicament. He scoffed at Job,

> If you sin, how does that affect him?
>   If your sins are many, what does that do to him?
> If you are righteous, what do you give to him,
>   or what does he receive from your hand?
> Your wickedness affects only a man like yourself,
>   and your righteousness only the sons of men. (35:6–8)

The opening chapters of Job, however, reveal that God staked a lot on one man's wickedness or righteousness. Somehow, in a way the book only suggests and does not explain, one person's faith made a difference. That, to me, is the most powerful and enduring lesson from the book of Job.

Like Job, we live in ignorance of what is going on "behind the curtains." Job reminds us that the small history of mankind on this earth—and, in fact, my own small history of faith—takes place within the large drama of the history of the universe. We are foot soldiers in a spiritual battle with cosmic significance. In the words of C. S. Lewis, "There is no neutral ground in the universe: every square inch, every split second, is claimed by God and counterclaimed by Satan."

For Job, the battleground of faith involved lost possessions, lost family members, lost health. We may face a different struggle: a career failure, a floundering marriage, sexual orientation, a face or body shape that turns people off, not on. Our own trials may not be the outgrowth of a cosmic contest waged in heaven. Regardless, the message of this book calls for the tough, hard-edged faith that believes, against the odds, that one person's response does indeed make a difference.

Job presents the astounding truth that our choices of faith matter not just to us and our own destiny but, amazingly, to God himself. Eliphaz taunted Job, "Can a man be of benefit to God? . . . What would he gain if your ways were blameless?" (22:1–3). At the end, Eliphaz may have chewed on those words as he offered sacrifices through Job and asked forgiveness. Job's faith gained for God a great victory over Satan, who had questioned the entire human experiment.

A piece of the history of the universe was at stake in Job and is still at stake in our own responses. The Bible gives hints, only hints, into the mystery behind that truth:

- A statement by Jesus in Luke 10 that while his followers were out announcing the kingdom of God, "I saw Satan fall like lightning from heaven."
- An intriguing whisper in Romans 8 that we on earth will be agents for redeeming nature. "The creation waits in eager expectation for the sons of God to be revealed" (8:19). Or, as Clarence Jordan's *Cotton Patch Version of Paul's Epistles* translates it, "In fact, the fondest dream of the universe is to catch a glimpse of real live sons and daughters of God."
- This phrase from Ephesians: "His intent was that now, through the church, the manifold wisdom of God should be made known to the rulers and authorities in the heavenly realms" (3:10).
- A sweeping assertion from the apostle Peter that "Even angels long to look into these things" (1 Peter 1:12).

Such veiled hints reiterate the central message of Job: How we respond *matters*. By hanging onto the thinnest thread of faith, Job won a crucial victory in God's grand plan to redeem the earth. In his grace, God has given ordinary men and women the dignity of participating in the redemption of the cosmos. He is allowing us, through our obedience to him, to help reverse the pain and unfairness of this world that Job described so eloquently. We might even say that God agrees with Job's complaints against the fallen world; God's plan to reverse the Fall depends on the faith of those who follow him.

You and I, in our mundane, personal struggles, serve as soldiers in that campaign. As William James put it in *The Will to Believe*, "Our present life *feels* like a real fight—as if there were something really wild in the universe which we, with all our idealities and faithfulnesses, are needed to redeem."

I have mentioned that Job represents a step beyond the reward/punishment "contract faith" assumed by the Israelites. The New Testament takes an even further step: its authors seem to *expect* suffering as a matter of course. "Christ suffered for you, leaving you an example, that you should follow in his steps" (1 Peter 2:21). Peter and ten others of Jesus' disciples went on to martyrs' deaths—hardly the "happy ending" suggested in the book of Job. Clearly, something changed in believers' expectations about suffering, and that change centered on the cross on which Jesus died.

Other passages explore this mystery, using phrases I will not attempt to explain. Paul speaks of "sharing in [Christ's] sufferings" and says he hopes to "fill up in my flesh what is still lacking in regard to Christ's afflictions." In context, such passages show that suffering can gain meaning if we consider it as part of the "cross" we take up in following Jesus. We become co-participants with Christ in the battle to expel evil from this planet, helping to accomplish God's redemptive purposes in the world.

We will never know, in this life, the full significance of our actions here for, as Job demonstrates, much takes place invisible to us. Jesus' cross offers a pattern for that too: what seemed very ordinary, one more dreary feat of colonial "justice" in a Roman outpost, made possible the salvation of the entire world.

In exaggerated form, Job affirms the mystery that, for whatever reason, God has given individual human beings a significant role to play in remaking a spoiled planet. When a pastor goes to prison for his peaceful protest against injustice, when a social worker moves into an urban ghetto in order to rebuild community from the ground up, when a couple refuses to give up on a difficult marriage, when a parent waits with undying hope and forgiveness for the return of an estranged child, when a son or daughter chooses to care for a terminally ill parent rather than investigate euthanasia, when a young professional resists mounting temptations toward wealth and success—in all these sufferings, large and small, there is the assurance of a deeper level of meaning, of a sharing in Christ's own redemptive victory. "The creation waits in eager expectation for the sons of God to be revealed" (Romans 8:19).

No one has expressed the pain and unfairness of this world any better than Job. Yet behind those words of anguish lies a darkly shining truth: Job—and you and I—can through obedience join the struggle to reverse that suffering. Job paints the drama of faith in its starkest form: the best man on earth suffering the worst, with no sign of encouragement or comfort from God. The fact that Job continued to trust God, against all odds, mattered—for him, for us, and for God. In his speech, God described the wonders of natural creation, yet clearly the wonder of creation that impressed God most was Job himself—hence this book in the Bible.

Thousands of years later, Job's questions have not gone away. People who suffer still find themselves borrowing Job's words as they cry out against God's apparent lack of concern. The book of Job affirms that God is not deaf to our cries and is in control of this world no matter how it appears. God did not answer all Job's questions, but God's very presence caused his doubts to melt away. Job learned that God cared about him intimately, and that God rules the world. That seemed enough.

Postscript

Job and the Riddles of Suffering

"But those who suffer he delivers in their suffering; he speaks to them in their affliction" (Job 36:15).

As I have said, Job raises more questions about suffering than it answers. Although the conclusion of the book, with its dramatic personal appearance by God himself, seems perfectly stage-managed for an enlightening monologue, God shuns the question. To complicate matters, various theories about the origin of suffering, fine-sounding theories proposed by Job's friends, God dismisses with a scowl.

The book of Job, an amazing account of very bad things happening to a very good man, thus contains no compact theory of why good people suffer. Nevertheless, it does offer many "over-the-shoulder" insights into the problem of pain. My own study has led me to the conclusions that follow. Although they do not answer the problem of pain—something not even God attempted—these principles may shed light on misconceptions that are as widespread today as in Job's time.

1. Chapters 1 and 2 make the subtle but important distinction that God did not directly cause Job's problems. He permitted them, but Satan actually caused the suffering.

2. Nowhere does the book of Job suggest that God lacks power or goodness. Some people (including Rabbi Kushner in his best-seller *When Bad Things Happen to Good People*) claim that a weak God lacks the power to prevent human suffering. Others deistically assume that God runs the world at a distance, without personal involvement. In contrast, the book of Job does not call into question God's power—only his fairness. Indeed, in the final summation speech God uses magnificent illustrations from nature to demonstrate his power.

3. Job decisively refutes one theory, that suffering always comes as a result of sin. The Bible supports the general principle

that "a man reaps what he sows," even in this life. But other people have no right to apply that general principle to a particular person. Job's friends persuasively argued that Job deserved such catastrophic punishment. When God rendered the final verdict, however, he said to them, "You have not spoken of me what is right, as my servant Job has" (42:7). Later, Jesus would also speak out against the notion that suffering automatically implies sin (see John 9:1–5 and Luke 13:1–5).

4. Having no clearly formed belief in an afterlife, Job's friends wrongly assumed that God's fairness—his approval or disapproval of people—had to be shown in this life only. Other parts of the Bible teach that God will mete out justice after death.

The pleasure that Job enjoyed in his old age is a mere foretaste of what is to come. The author of Job 42 includes one poignant detail. All of Job's material possessions are doubled in his old age. Once owner of 7,000 sheep, 3,000 camels, 500 yoke of oxen, and 500 donkeys, he now possesses 14,000 sheep, 6,000 camels, 1,000 yoke of oxen, and 1,000 donkeys. Significantly, though, his family does not double. The father of seven sons and three daughters becomes father of seven new sons and three new daughters—not fourteen sons and six daughters. Even in the middle of the Old Testament, which has a shadowy concept of the afterlife at best, the book of Job clearly intimates that Job will one day get his original family back. The ten children he tragically lost will be restored to him, to live in glorious eternity in a redeemed and recreated world.

5. God did not condemn Job's doubt and despair, only his ignorance. The phrase "the patience of Job" hardly fits the stream of invective that poured from Job's mouth. Job did not take his pain meekly; he cried out in protest to God. His strong remarks scandalized his friends but not God. Need we worry about somehow insulting God with an outburst triggered by stress or pain? Not according to this book. In a touch of

supreme irony, God ordered Job's friends to seek repentance from Job himself, the object of their pious condescension.

6. No one has all the facts about suffering. Job concluded he was righteous and God was being unfair. His friends insisted on the opposite: God was righteous and Job was being rightfully punished. Ultimately, all of them learned they had been viewing the situation from a limited perspective, blind to the real struggle being waged in heaven.

7. God is never totally silent. Elihu made that point convincingly, reminding Job of dreams, visions, past blessings, even the daily works of God in nature (chapter 33). God also appealed to nature as giving evidence of his wisdom and power. Although God may seem silent, some sign of him can still be found. Author Joseph Bayly expressed the truth this way: "Remember in the darkness what you have learned in the light."

8. Well-intentioned advice may sometimes do more harm than good. The behavior of Job's friends gives a classic example of how pride and a sense of being right can stifle true compassion. The friends repeated pious phrases and argued theology with Job, insisting on their wrong-headed notions about suffering (notions that still abound). Job's response: "If only you would be altogether silent! For you, that would be wisdom" (13:4, 5). As it turned out, the most compassionate thing the friends did for Job took place at the very beginning, when they sat in silence with him for seven days.

9. God re-focused the central issue from the *cause* of Job's suffering to his *response*. Mysteriously, God never gave his own explanation of the problem of suffering, nor did he inform Job of the contest recorded in chapters 1 and 2. The real issue at stake was Job's faith: whether he would continue to trust God even when everything went wrong. By instinct we tend to focus on the "Why?" question; God seems more interested in "To what end?" Once suffering has happened, bad as it is, can it somehow be used for good?

10. Suffering, in God's plan, can be redeemed, or serve a higher good. In Job's case, a period of great travail was used by God to win an important, even cosmic, victory. Looking backward—but only looking backward—we can see the "advantage" Job gained by continuing to trust God. Through his undeserved suffering, the righteous man Job gave an "advance echo" of Jesus Christ, who would live a perfect life, yet endure pain and death in order to win a great victory.

THREE

Deuteronomy:
A Taste of Bittersweet

THREE

Deuteronomy: A Taste of Bittersweet

There are two tragedies in life. One is to lose your heart's desire.
The other is to gain it.

—GEORGE BERNARD SHAW

When Communism fell in 1989, small countries in Eastern
Europe and Central Asia suddenly found themselves free of the
long shadow of the Soviet Union. No one gave them orders
anymore. No one imposed policies. On their own they had to
figure out how to design a flag, train an army, manage foreign
affairs, settle border disputes—in short, how to run a country.
Each nation's success or failure depended on what kind of
leader emerged from the Cold War thaw.

Czechoslovakia instinctively turned to Václav Havel, a playwright who had spent years in prison for his political dissent.
Although Havel had no experience and little interest in politics,
he accepted the daunting task of fashioning a new, free country. To connect with his people, he began a practice that became
a tradition: each week he appeared on television to answer
callers' questions. He explained how the new government
would work, reviewed the budget, discussed controversial new
laws, lectured on morality and responsibility. At times preacher,
cheerleader, historian, and coach, this playwright-intellectual
against all odds became a media star, presiding over one of the

most popular shows in the country. By sheer eloquence and force of personality Havel ushered the Czech people through a painful split with Slovakia and prepared them for life as an independent nation. It felt, he said, like a parent trying to teach an unruly bunch of children how to behave as adults.

In a nutshell, that is the situation Moses confronted toward the end of his life. A reluctant leader who had spent forty years tending sheep in a wilderness, he was abruptly called by God to emancipate the Hebrews from the most powerful empire in the world. Moses did that and more, coaxing and cajoling the freed slaves through four decades of immaturity in the Sinai desert. Now, just as Moses' own life was ending, the Hebrews stood at the threshold of the Promised Land, eager to take the reins of nationhood.

Moses had one last shot, one last opportunity to pass along historical memory, to purge himself of grievances and pain, to bequeath to them the hope and grit they would desperately need in his absence. To his people, he represented not only a trailblazer like Václav Havel; he was the Liberator—Simón Bolívar, Nelson Mandela, Mahatma Gandhi, and George Washington all pressed into one frail old body.

"If the various writers of the Bible were composers, the Deuteronomist would be Bach in his utter, majestic confidence," writes Jack Miles. Deuteronomy stands as the last of the five "books of Moses," the grand summation, the first full-blown oratory in the Bible, and the record of Moses' final words to the children of Israel. In forty torturous years a stuttering shepherd, shy of leadership and haunted by his crime of passion, has become one of the giants of history whose achievements changed the planet forever. Deuteronomy gives Moses' own account of that remarkable transformation.

The old man clutches his robe and shivers in spite of the desert heat. Assistants help him scrabble up the tallest rock. Before him, stretching all the way to the horizon, are the Israelites. He pauses to let the cheers of the crowd die down. His eyes lock onto a few anonymous faces. So young, so innocent. None of them has a single memory of the glories of Egypt, the fabulous land of pyramids and palaces and chariots. These desert kids know only the rigors of Sinai: scorpions, vipers, blazing heat, cold nights, sandstorms, the endless search for water.

None of their parents have survived, save two. The rest proved useless. He dragged them out of Egypt only to find they had kept Egypt inside them. Now he faces their eager young descendants, a nation intact but with all its individual cells replaced. Children, that's what they are, mere children. He'd give anything to lead them across the river into the land he's been crowing about for forty years. He sighs, with a sound more like a groan. It won't work, he knows. Instead, he'll die here, maybe even today. They'll be alone soon, this brood of the desert. He's gathered them together to say farewell.

Like a hive of bees, the mob buzzes with energy. Moses hasn't seen such excitement since the day their parents walked out of Egypt loaded down with the gold of the pharaohs. How quickly the smiles left their faces; how long will they last on these children's? They have heard stories from their parents, he knows—the same parents who grumbled, complained, and outright rebelled against his leadership. This is his last chance to set the record straight, to right the blame and the credit, to get history down not just for these children but for all to follow, for all posterity.

Moses' eyes are the color of clotted milk. Eighty years in the desert have carved walrus wrinkles across his face. The sounds of the multitude blend together into a low, irritating hum. Joshua and Caleb, trusted associates, have quieted the throng and are motioning for him to begin. They've arranged for "shouters" to repeat his words, projecting them out so everyone can hear. "Speak slowly," they advise. "Take your time." But as he begins to speak, his voice cracks and the old stutter starts up again.

Moses is the oldest person any of the Israelites have seen, the only truly ancient person among them, nearly twice the age of Joshua and Caleb. With his snow-white hair and flowing beard, he seems more mythological creature than man. He has dominated their lives from birth. They have heard how he strode past guards in the great pharaoh's palace and surprised the ruler who was once his playmate. The plagues, so traumatic at the time, over the years have become the fodder of jokes: frogs jumping through the kitchen, gnats and flies swarming the soldiers and foremen, boils forcing the Egyptian magicians to roll naked in the sand for relief. Moses the magician stage-managed all that.

Their parents used to speak longingly of the palm trees, the houses piled atop one another so high as to block the sun, the streets crowded with chariots, donkey carts, and long caravans of camels. Of such this throng has no memory. They have only the hope of a new start, a nation where they will serve as masters and not slaves, a land not desiccated but lush with pastures and crops, a land they can call their own.

Moses' life had a single theme: God did it. How many times had his mother recounted the tale of his miraculous survival during the Pharaoh's campaign to exterminate Hebrew babies? "God saved you, Moses," she told him over and over. "He has something very special in mind for you." She laughed that proud mother's laugh as she reminded him that God arranged for her, his birth mother, to get a royal pension for nursing him. Meanwhile he played in the courts of Pharaoh, acquired a superb classical education, and dined with the elite of the empire.

Secretly knowing his true identity, Moses felt like a person without a country. When other Egyptian princes told crude jokes about the Hebrew slaves, he bit his tongue. When his own people, the Hebrews, taunted him for his uppity manners and palace accent, he bit his tongue again. He loved both families, birth and adopted. He never tired of the peasant family dinners, followed by the old men rehashing the stories of Abraham, Isaac, and Jacob and the God they still worshiped despite the fact that he seemed to have fallen asleep for a dozen generations. Moses especially loved the story of Joseph. "You could be a new Joseph," said his mother as she kissed him goodbye one night. "You too walk in Pharaoh's palace. God may use you to help save us."

On the other hand, he could not imagine life without the training he got every day among the smartest students in the empire. He loved the sports competitions, the feasts, the fine wine, the oiled and perfumed women who taught him art and music. Like a spy, he balanced the two worlds successfully, keeping them in sealed compartments and flourishing in both— until one day the two collided and he had to choose between them.

At the time it seemed a simple matter of justice. Dressed in the full regalia of an Egyptian prince, a gold headpiece and buckle announcing his office, he visited a work site of the Pharaoh. There he saw a mid-level Egyptian foreman savagely beating a Hebrew, one of Moses' countrymen. He gave the tyrant a shove, finished him off, and hid the corpse in the sand, then went on as if nothing had happened. Others had seen the deed, though, and now the cat had escaped the bag.

On that day at the work site, Moses realized what side he was truly on. Egyptians used the word *Hapiru* as a term of scorn for Hebrews: "the dusty ones." If an Egyptian dies, of course someone must pay. But if one of the Hapiru dies, who cares? I care, Moses decided. They may be slaves, but they are my kinsmen. No one deserves this treatment.

To Pharaoh, Moses had crossed a line and got caught on the wrong side. He could not tolerate insurrection. It was he, after all, who had ordered the infanticide campaign against Moses' tribe. Pharaoh issued a death warrant for the impostor prince named Moses.

A fugitive, Moses fled Egypt and for forty years had no contact with either of his families. A new life began that surprisingly suited him, the lonely life of a nomad. He gained a wife, an extended family, and a new set of wilderness survival skills. Out of prudence Moses said little to anyone about his past and had little reason to. No one in Midian cared about the Hebrews, nor about the Egyptians for that matter. His world gradually shrank into a circle of domestic tranquility, and at the ripe old age of eighty he concerned himself mainly with children, in-laws, and sheep.

God, however, had other plans. While Moses was forging a new life in Midian, far from the Hebrew slaves, God had been listening to their groans. All at once the slow, mysterious work of a timeless God came into sharp focus, revealing that nothing in Moses' circuitous life had been wasted. God now had a Hebrew of pure pedigree, expertly trained in Egyptian leadership skills, fully capable of surviving in the wilderness. The time for liberation of God's chosen people had arrived. Now to convince Moses. And Pharaoh.

Moses raised powerful objections to God's plans. First, there was the question of his trustworthiness. Why should the Hebrews trust someone trained by the enemy, let alone a fugitive who had skipped the country for forty years? Besides, both the Hebrews and Pharaoh would need an articulate leader to stir them into action—why pick someone with a stutter? "O Lord, please send someone else," Moses begged. A few words spoken from a burning bush silenced Moses; convincing Pharaoh was another matter.

Thus did a diffident shepherd become the first intermediary chosen by God to speak to his people, and also the first person recorded in the Bible to work miracles. Moses' initial fears proved accurate, however. After an Egyptian crackdown doubled their workload, the Hebrews abandoned Moses and his brother Aaron. The Israelites were supposed to believe that a God absent for four hundred years had suddenly decided to take on the Pharaoh and his armies? Dream on.

Moses did not even have the support of his own people as he strode up the massive stone steps to Pharaoh's palace, its gold finials gleaming in the desert sun. He looked around. The Pharaoh had nearly finished his grand construction plans. A city of white limestone, more dazzling than the sun, had grown up around the drab buildings he knew as a boy.

Hieroglyphics carved into the stone walls said it all. Unused in forty years, Moses' first language came flooding back as he studied the accounts of Pharaoh's military conquests. He felt a stab of pain as he recognized the Egyptian symbol for foreigner: a bound man with blood flowing from a wound in his head. The wilderness of Midian had rid him of all nostalgia for the luxuries of Egypt. Sumptuous banquets, orgies, pretentious dress with social rank carefully scripted in hair, armbands, and clothing styles—all this seemed a stench to him now. He knew his proper identity: a foreigner; an alien in a strange land; a *Gershom*, the very name he had chosen for his son. His people, the Hebrews, were the bound ones with blood flowing from their wounds: the Hapiru, the dusty ones who worked in the mud and bore the lashes of the Egyptians. Their only hope, only future, now rested in God's hands alone.

Why on earth would my appointment secretary admit this smelly goatherd? thought Pharaoh on seeing but not yet recognizing Moses. The uncouth visitor whispered his words of introduction to Aaron, his interpreter, but no one could understand Aaron's rustic speech. When Moses himself finally spoke up, all the attendants drew back at the sound. Out of the rube's mouth flowed perfect, aristocratic Egyptian.

A few minutes later Moses the former prince of Egypt and Pharaoh the ruling king were laughing together over the good old days. The Pharaoh's gold necklaces and bracelets jangled as he clapped his hands in joy. To the guards' astonishment, he even allowed the coarse visitor to touch him!

The two had once been playmates, before Moses had crossed the reigning Pharaoh. But the old man, long dead, was now resting in unimaginable splendor in the Valley of the Kings. "We put enough food and furniture in his tomb to keep him in comfort for eternity," said the new Pharaoh, his son. "Already I have fifty thousand workmen preparing my own tomb. You can never be too careful."

Anything Moses wanted, he could have—for himself, that is, not for the rest of the Hebrews. "Think about it, Moses. Put yourself in my place. No monarch would let his main work force just walk away. I have cities to build, and aqueducts, and forts." Though the Pharaoh did not say it, they both knew the Hebrew slaves did all the dirty work, at minimal cost. "Come back to the palace and enjoy life," he urged. "Don't worry about the incident at the construction site. Just as Father promised, I am now Egypt—the morning and the evening star. If I say day is night, it will be so written. Join me and forget the Hebrews."

God had not forgotten the Hebrews, however: "I have seen the oppression of my people in Egypt and have heard their cry," he told Moses from the burning bush. Neither could Moses forget his people. At one time Pharaoh's offer might have tempted him, but not now. He looked back in shame on the days when he called "Father" the man who had slaughtered the Hebrew children. After forty years in the wilderness, he had been unprepared for the sight of slave labor again. It felt like a kick in the gut. Moses in effect flung down a gauntlet, challenging the mightiest empire in the world to a form of cosmic combat, with the very heavens choosing sides.

Soon Moses and the Pharaoh were engaged in a great tug-of-war, not so different from the games they used to play in the courtyards although now with stakes raised higher. "I will not be dictated to! I will not be threatened!" shouted the Pharaoh in a tone Moses had never before heard. "I am the morning and the evening star. I am Pharaoh!"

Egypt and its mighty gods stood in splendid array against the invisible God of the Hebrews. To the Egyptians, the Hebrews' notion of a single, invisible God seemed ludicrous. They worshiped an elaboration of gods who could be visually celebrated in the splendid temples: Horus the hawk, Thot the ibis, Khunm the ram, Apis the sacred bull. Each possessed mysterious characteristics known only to the priests. What good was a god you could not see or even represent in sculpture or painting?

As for the Hebrews' request to withdraw into the desert to offer sacrifices, that seemed an obvious escape ploy. Did not the temple of Karnak down the river employ 70,000 full-time priests and acolytes? If the Hebrews wanted to sacrifice, why not hire the experts?

Yet one by one the Egyptian gods fell to the plagues unleashed by Moses' God: the river god turned to blood, the sacred fly became a swarming pest, the sun-god Ra disappeared behind a cloud, the great bull failed to protect his livestock. Finally, in the last and worst plague, the Pharaoh, along with every other Egyptian, lost his firstborn son. At last he conceded defeat; the invisible God had won. The very next day Hebrew slaves, loaded down with Egyptian plunder, walked away in a huge, ragtag mob, at the head of which marched Moses, Prince of Israel.

Moses himself would have resisted the title, of course. From the moment he first saw the bush that would not stop burning, he had learned one lesson above all others: the mission was God's, not his. Moses merely played the role God assigned him. He tried to drum that lesson into the Israelites every year at Passover, when they remembered that last, murderous night in Egypt, when no Israelite armies faced the mighty Egyptians. Freedom came in the blackest night while Hebrew families huddled around the Passover table, their bags packed, waiting for deliverance. God alone did it. Later, when the Pharaoh changed his mind and set his chariots loose upon the fleeing tribes, and all the Israelites whimpered like cowards, God came through again. God even designated the Exodus as a way of describing himself: "I am the God who brought you out of Egypt."

That same pattern of abject dependence would continue all through the wilderness wanderings. When the Hebrews ran out of water, God provided. When food supplies failed, God provided. When raiders attacked, God provided. Liberation was God's act, and he alone deserved the credit.

Years of sheep-herding during his exile in Midian had mellowed Moses, preparing him for his leadership role in the Sinai. In the old days he took matters into his own hands. All three scenes from his youth involved violence: murdering an Egyptian foreman, breaking up a fight among his brethren, chasing a bunch of shepherds away from some vulnerable women (and impressing his future wife in the process). Now the famous temper had softened.

Once only did it rear up strongly enough to defy God himself: when Moses smashed his walking stick against a rock in anger. "You want water? I'll give you water!" he had screamed at the thirsty whiners. That lapse cost him the dream of his life, the chance to set foot in the Promised Land. For a moment

Moses forgot it was God's work, not his own, and for this reason he now stood on the tall rock before the anxious multitude on the wrong side of the Jordan river.

Keep it positive, old man, he mumbles to himself. Remember, this is their big day. Don't take it away from them. It was their parents who angered God, not these kids here today. Give them hope. Let them celebrate.

Try as he might, he cannot help lashing out. Footsore and weary, as he thinks back over the last third of his life, all he feels is disappointment. "You are too heavy a burden for me to carry alone," he says and waits for the shouters to repeat it. Well, it's true, they are a burden—a bleating, squirming mess of ingrates he has pulled across the desert like a donkey dragging a cart up a mountain. No sooner had he got them out of Egypt than they started pining for the fruits and spices they left behind. Ingrates! God gives them manna and they want steak. God makes rocks bleed water and they beg for rivers.

They're stiff-necked, like the ox that used to resist his yoking in Midian. Unless the stupid beast relaxed, he could never get the yoke to settle tight across its neck. The dumb ox wore sores all day because of its own stubbornness. This tribe has been wandering for forty years in a wilderness with a yoke bouncing up and down their stiff necks. It should have taken eleven days, the miserable journey, not forty years.

"You were unwilling to go up; you rebelled against the command of the Lord your God. You grumbled in your tents. . . . You have been rebellious against the Lord ever since I have known you."

Easy, old man. Let it go. Remember, these are kids standing here. Their parents did all that, not these kids. But he can't help it. He's got forty years worth of bile to unload, and the parents are no longer here to dump it on.

"Because of you the Lord became angry with me also and said, 'You shall not enter it, either.'" That's what really sticks in his craw. How come these kids get to prance into the land of milk and honey while the great liberator, the one who bore them like a burden, who stuck up for them when even God abandoned them, has to stand at the very edge of happiness . . . and die. It's not fair. None of it is fair. "I told you, but you would not listen. You rebelled against the Lord's command. . . ."

The speech is not going well. Moses can sense it in the crowd: the women talking among themselves, the men looking down and shuffling their feet, the children drifting off to play. This is his last shot, and he's blowing it. Still, doesn't he have a right to his say? Hasn't he earned it? Who cares how they respond right now. They've got to listen. One day they'll understand. One day they'll know how much they hurt him.

"I pleaded with the Lord, 'Let me go over and see the good land beyond the Jordan—that fine hill country and Lebanon.' But because of you the Lord was angry with me and would not listen to me."

No doubt the crowd understood the dyspeptic raves of the old man. Every last one of their parents lay buried in the Sinai sand and soon Moses would join them, a shabby end to his life of service. He had known few joys, and surely they had not made it easy, bringing him their long list of problems each day. They had gossiped about him, mistrusted him, envied him. No one really liked Moses—how can you relate to such a man, forty years your senior, a man who prefers tending sheep to tending people, who meets with God alone in a tent?—and he must have known it.

It was a long speech Moses gave, three speeches in all, and despite his tendency to lapse into rancor against his own ill fortune, he did pull himself together enough to get across the main message, which could be summarized in one word: Remember! With the speeches in Deuteronomy, Moses established the great tradition of historical memory, a tradition his people, who became known as the Jews, have cherished ever since: "Never forget." Try as we might, we can never undo the past, but still we must honor it by bearing witness, by remembering so as not to allow it to repeat.

One would think in view of all that had transpired—the centuries of slavery, the Ten Plagues, the Red Sea miracle, the victories over surrounding tribes—the Hebrews would not need such a pedantic reminder. Forget God one generation after the Exodus? How could they ever again doubt such a God? Yet Moses knew by intuition that the simple act of remembering would require daily acts of concentration.

> Be careful that you do not forget the Lord your God, failing to observe his commands, his laws and his decrees that I am giving you this day. Otherwise, when you eat and are satisfied, when you build fine houses and settle down, and when your herds and flocks grow large and your silver and gold increase and all you have is multiplied, then your heart will become proud and you will forget the Lord your God, who brought you out of Egypt, out of the land of slavery. He led you through the vast and dreadful desert, that thirsty and waterless land, with its venomous snakes and scorpions. He brought you water out of hard rock. He gave you manna to eat in the desert, something your fathers had never known, to humble and to test you so that in the end it might go well with you. You may say to yourself, "My power and the strength of my hands have produced this wealth for me." But remember the Lord your God, for it is he who gives

you the ability to produce wealth, and so confirms his covenant, which he swore to your forefathers, as it is today.

Nothing, apparently, bothers God more than the simple act of being forgotten. During the years of wilderness wanderings, forced to depend on God daily, the Hebrews did not have the luxury of forgetting. God fed the Israelites, clothed them, planned their daily itinerary, and fought their battles. No Hebrew questioned the existence of God in those days, for he hovered before them in a thick cloud and a pillar of fire.

Soon, however, God would withdraw from that smothering parental role. On the first day they ate produce from the Promised Land, the manna would stop. From then on they must cultivate their own land and plant their own crops. They would build cities, fight wars, appoint a king. They would prosper and grow plump. They would trust their armies and chariots instead of their God, forgetting the lesson inflicted on almighty Egypt. They would discriminate against the poor and the aliens, forgetting they were once both. In a word, they would forget God.

> These commandments that I give you today are to be upon your hearts. Impress them on your children. Talk about them when you sit at home and when you walk along the road, when you lie down and when you get up. Tie them as symbols on your hands and bind them on your foreheads. Write them on the doorframes of your houses and on your gates.
>
> When the Lord your God brings you into the land he swore to your fathers, to Abraham, Isaac and Jacob, to give you—a land with large, flourishing cities you did not build, houses filled with all kinds of good things you did not provide, wells you did not dig, and vineyards and olive groves you did not plant—then when you eat and are satisfied, be careful that you do not forget the

Lord, who brought you out of Egypt, out of the land of slavery.

Success, not failure, is the greatest danger facing any follower of God, as Moses knew well. He had traipsed around a desert for forty years as a penalty for the Hebrews' inability to handle the success of the Exodus. Every significant downfall in his own life came when he seized power for himself—killing an Egyptian, smashing a rock in the desert—rather than relying on God.

In contrast, perhaps his greatest military victory came when he played an almost slapstick role. No general at the head of his troops, Moses stood apart, atop a nearby hill, raising his hands high like a religious zealot. As long as he reached out toward God, the Israelites won; whenever his hands sank down, the Amalekites won. By the end of the day an exhausted Moses was sitting on a rock with each up-stretched arm supported by a helper. God's strength is perfected in weakness.

Somehow, just talking about the bitterness softens it a little. There have surely been good times, Moses reminds himself. He's had God by his side each step of the way, and even when it feels as if God alone supports him, that is enough. The time when Korah and the gang rebelled against him—in the old days he would have grabbed a sword and run them through. Instead, he simply waited for God to settle it. Later, when his own siblings turned against him and mocked his African wife, then too he stood aside and let God work out the justice. And God did, giving Aaron and Miriam the dressing down of their lives. "With him I speak face to face," God said of Moses in a voice like thunder. "How dare you speak against my servant?" Moses had hung his head and blushed.

Once, Moses overheard someone talking about "the meekest man on the face of the earth," and to his astonishment he learned they were talking about him! His mother and Pharaoh would certainly never have used that description, Moses had chuckled to himself. Probably not God either. Meek? Humble? Imagine.

Over the years Moses has learned something so sweet and strange and mysterious that only one word can begin to capture it: *grace*, God's free, undeserved gift. He has learned that God loves him despite his failures, with a pure, stubborn, everlasting love. After more than a century of life, Moses has given up trying to figure out what God sees in him. Or sees in the rest of the Hebrews for that matter. He just accepts it and gives thanks.

Moses takes a long draught of water from a goatskin bag, moistens his lips, clears the phlegm from his throat. "Listen up. Pay attention. Here's what I want you to remember. Even if you forget everything else I say, think on this." Another pause, another swallow. The crowd stills, detecting a change in Moses' voice. An expression of bliss crosses his face so that it almost glows. They know that expression; they've seen it whenever Moses emerged from the sacred tent after his meetings with God.

> The Lord did not set his affection on you and choose you because you were more numerous than other peoples, for you were the fewest of all peoples. But it was because the Lord loved you and kept the oath he swore to your forefathers that he brought you out with a mighty hand and redeemed you from the land of slavery, from the power of Pharaoh king of Egypt. Know, therefore, that the Lord your God is God; he is the faithful God, keeping his covenant of love to a thousand generations of those who love him and keep his commands.

He is warming to the message now, his weary voice ascending in both pitch and volume.

To the Lord your God belong the heavens, even the highest heavens, the earth and everything in it. Yet the Lord set his affection on your forefathers and loved them, and he chose you, their descendants, above all the nations, as it is today. . . . He is your praise; he is your God, who performed for you those great and awesome wonders you saw with your own eyes. Your forefathers who went down into Egypt were seventy in all, and now the Lord your God has made you as numerous as the stars in the sky.

"As the stars in the sky"—he likes that. Didn't God promise as much to Abraham? Now here it is, prophecy fulfilled before his very eyes. They may have murmured and rebelled and driven the older generation to an early grave, but here they stand, the Israelites, God's chosen people, his "peculiar treasures" assembled at the very border of a new land.

He drinks again from the goatskin bag, letting the words sink in. They are responding to the positive tone. Who doesn't want to hear that God loves them?

The first time Moses encountered God up-close it took his breath away. He hid his face in shame and fear. Yet after forty years of such encounters, he and God have grown to be—could he say it?—friends. He argues with God, even bargains with him. He loses sometimes, as with his request to enter the Promised Land, but sometimes he wins, like the time God nearly called off the whole project until Moses talked him out of it.

Moses ignores his notes and begins to ramble, reminding the crowd of that, his finest hour. Three days' journey from Egypt and they were complaining about the water; a month later they had forgotten the bullwhips and were mewling about Egypt's figs and pomegranates; then, a month after that, the holiest moment in Moses' life, he descended from the cloud to find a scene that made him retch. He had been meeting with God on the sacred mountain, getting the stone tablets inscribed by God's own hand. When he came down, his face shining like a lantern, he found them cavorting around a golden calf, an Egyptian idol. It was too much. He would have divorced his people on the spot had not God reached that decision first.

Suddenly Moses was the only thing preventing the annihilation of every last Hebrew. God meant business. Moses threw the sacred tablets to the ground, shattering them, then threw himself down. He lay there prostrate for forty days and forty nights, a day's penance for each day he had spent with God on the holy mountain. He ate no bread and drank no water, and all day long the Hebrews warily circled his still body, wondering if he had died, wondering if they would now die. They certainly would have, had Moses not pleaded their case before God.

"Leave me alone so that my anger may burn against them and that I may destroy them. Then I will make you into a great nation." A tempting offer God made him. But Moses would not leave God alone. He argued, pleaded, whined. He appealed to God's mercy, to his pride, to his reputation. He begged God to take him, Moses, instead and let the others live. He reminded God of his favorites: Abraham, Isaac, and Jacob. At last God relented. He allowed Moses to see a visible glimpse of him such that no one on earth had ever seen. He made a new covenant, agreeing to accompany his people to the Promised Land.

Though reared among the Egyptians and their animal-shaped gods, Moses rediscovered a fundamental fact about God forgotten during the four hundred years of silence: God is a person. During the years of silence, the Hebrews thought of God, if at all, as a distant, unapproachable, ineffable mystery who showed little concern over what was transpiring on earth.

Moses reminded the Hebrews that God is as personal as they themselves; indeed their own "personhood" was a faint reflection of what God is like.

When God makes a list of commandments, *Love* takes first place, the basis of his whole relationship with humanity. God meets in a tent and discusses policy, as a man speaks to a friend. He listens, and he argues back. God also feels pain. When jilted, God suffers like any wounded lover. He makes threats, then backs down from them. He negotiates and signs contracts.

This last fact, above all, separated the Hebrews from their neighbors. Even the haughty Egyptians lived in fear of their capricious gods. The Canaanites sacrificed children to appease their unpredictable gods. But the God of the Hebrews proved willing to sign a contract detailing exactly what he expected from his people, and what he promised in return.

Except for Orthodox Jews, not many people today devote time to the legal code recorded in Exodus, Leviticus, and Deuteronomy. The laws seem repetitious and generally irrelevant to modern society. Yet, as Deuteronomy shows most clearly, these laws simply set the boundaries of a vastly unequal relationship: between an awesome, holy God and an ordinary people prone to failure and rebellion.

Years later, Moses knew, some would question specific laws in the contract. Moses anticipated such a question:

> In the future, when your son asks you, "What is the meaning of the stipulations, decrees and laws the Lord our God has commanded you?" tell him: "We were slaves of Pharaoh in Egypt, but the Lord brought us out of Egypt with a mighty hand. Before our eyes the Lord sent miraculous signs and wonders—great and terrible—upon Egypt and Pharaoh and his whole household. But he brought us out from there to bring us in and give us the land that he promised on oath to our forefathers. The Lord commanded us to obey all these decrees and to fear

the Lord our God, so that we might always prosper and be kept alive, as is the case today. And if we are careful to obey all this law before the Lord our God, as he has commanded us, that will be our righteousness."

In short, God gave the laws for the Hebrews' own good. Their prosperity, their very survival depended on this contract. Moses spelled out God's end of the bargain in vivid detail. Israelite wives would have many babies, all their crops would produce bountifully, cattle and sheep would multiply. He even included this extraordinary promise: "The Lord will keep you free from every disease." For the Israelites to receive these benefits, God asked only one thing in return—a big thing, as it turned out: follow the covenant agreement set forth in the contract.

God had an unprecedented relationship with the band of refugees who roamed the Sinai for forty years. Moses, for one, could not seem to get over it: "Ask from one end of the heavens to the other. Has anything so great as this ever happened, or has anything like it ever been heard of? Has any god ever tried to take for himself one nation out of another nation … like … the Lord your God did for you in Egypt before your very eyes?"

Later, the nation would go through Job-like times that called the contract itself into doubt. Their faith would confront questions of unfairness and feelings of abandonment. Now, however, at this moment, the wondrous plan was being fulfilled. God the sovereign chooser, the steadfast promise-maker, was bringing his chosen people into the Promised Land.

Moses' voice is tiring. He pauses more and more frequently. There is so little time. When he began the speech, he had the feeling he could stave off death by talking on and on. Now he hardly cares. Fatigue has numbed life. He has said it all and more, rambling, repeating, sometimes breaking down in tears in all the wrong places.

What, really, will they remember? Scribes are writing down the words for posterity, but against the enemies the Hebrews will soon meet, words make frail allies.

An idea. Back in Egypt they used stones for monuments. On columns, obelisks, and rock walls they wrote of Pharaoh's exploits and recorded the laws of the empire. When a criminal pled ignorance, they merely dragged him to the stone and pointed to the law he had broken. What if the Hebrews do that?

"Do it!" Moses commands. "When you have crossed the Jordan into the land the Lord your God is giving you, set up some large stones and coat them with plaster. Write on them all the words of this law . . . And when you have crossed the Jordan, set up these stones on Mount Ebal, as I command you today, and coat them with plaster."

A start, at least. What else? How can he impress on these people the meaning of a contract with God Almighty? Another idea. Moses assigns the tribe of Levites to shout out the laws. "Cursed is the man who moves his neighbor's boundary stone," they yell. Then all the people must say, "Amen!" so they'll have no excuse. Make them ratify this covenant point by point, aloud.

Next Moses appoints two antiphonal "choirs." They carry no melody but the discordant tones of the words they shout. Across the Jordan River, two mountains form a natural amphitheater. On Mount Gerizim six tribes of "optimists" will stand to recite the blessings.

> The Lord will grant that the enemies who rise up against you will be defeated before you. They will come at you from one direction but flee from you in seven.
> The Lord will open the heavens, the storehouse of his bounty, to send rain on your land in season and to bless all the

work of your hands. You will lend to many nations but will borrow from none. The Lord will make you the head, not the tail.
If you pay attention to the commands of the Lord your God
that I give you this day and carefully follow them, you will
always be at the top, never at the bottom.

More assurances along that line: victory in war, good
weather, a boom economy, health, prosperity. Every leader
promises such, of course, but in this case God himself has signed
the contract. That should make an impression.

Knowing these people, they'll need some warnings as well.
Many more warnings, in fact. Let loose with the curses. Don't hold
back; let the curses rain down. Blast away. Scare the sin out of them.

The Lord will strike you with wasting disease, with fever and
inflammation, with scorching heat and drought, with blight and
mildew, which will plague you until you perish. The sky over
your head will be bronze, the ground beneath you iron. The
Lord will turn the rain of your country into dust and powder;
it will come down from the skies until you are destroyed.

The Lord will cause you to be defeated before your enemies. You will come at them from one direction but flee from
them in seven, and you will become a thing of horror to all the
kingdoms on earth. Your carcasses will be food for all the birds
of the air and the beasts of the earth, and there will be no one
to frighten them away. The Lord will afflict you with the boils
of Egypt and with tumors, festering sores and the itch, from
which you cannot be cured. The Lord will afflict you with mad-
ness, blindness and confusion of mind. At midday you will
grope about like a blind man in the dark. You will be unsuc-
cessful in everything you do; day after day you will be
oppressed and robbed, with no one to rescue you.

God, could it be? Could you possibly abandon your people
like this? Moses sees it so clearly that his knees sag and his heart

skips beats. But he can hardly believe these things will happen to the people God loves.

> All these curses will come upon you. . . . Because you did not serve the Lord your God joyfully and gladly in the time of prosperity, therefore in hunger and thirst, in nakedness and dire poverty, you will serve the enemies the Lord sends against you.
>
> Because of the suffering that your enemy will inflict on you during the siege, you will eat the fruit of the womb, the flesh of the sons and daughters the Lord your God has given you. Even the most gentle and sensitive man among you will have no compassion on his own brother or the wife he loves or his surviving children, and he will not give to one of them any of the flesh of his children that he is eating. It will be all he has left because of the suffering your enemy will inflict on you during the siege of all your cities. The most gentle and sensitive woman among you—so sensitive and gentle that she would not venture to touch the ground with the sole of her foot—will begrudge the husband she loves and her own son or daughter the afterbirth from her womb and the children she bears. For she intends to eat them secretly during the siege and in the distress that your enemy will inflict on you in your cities.

He sees the enemy siege as if it is happening before him. He sees the piles of bodies, the parents fighting over their children's corpses, the beautiful Jewish maidens turned into haggard witches. Oh, if only his eyes would fail and spare him this sight. If only the Hebrews would go deaf and not hear these curses. But they must, they must. Knowing is their only chance of preventing.

> Then the Lord will scatter you among all nations, from one end of the earth to the other. . . . There the Lord will give you an anxious mind, eyes weary with longing, and a despairing heart. You will live in constant suspense, filled with dread both night and day, never sure of your life. In the morning you will say, "If only it were evening!" and in the evening, "If only it were morning!"—

because of the terror that will fill your hearts and the sights that your eyes will see. The Lord will send you back in ships to Egypt on a journey I said you should never make again. There you will offer yourselves for sale to your enemies as male and female slaves, but no one will buy you.

Moses cannot go on. What else can he say? A horror grips him as he sounds the words: the horror of truth. His voice has fallen to a whisper. What he delivers as dire warnings to keep his people from sin are, he knows, direct prophecies. He is giving an advance history of a people who will break their covenant with God, not once but time and again.

"See, I set before you today life and prosperity, death and destruction," Moses cries, almost shrieking into the air that has grown suddenly still. "This day I call heaven and earth as witnesses against you that I have set before you life and death, blessings and curses. Now choose life! For the Lord is your life."

More than anything, God longed for the covenant with the Hebrews to succeed: "Oh, that their hearts would be inclined to fear me and keep all my commands always, so that it might go well with them and their children forever!" he told Moses. The repeated rebellions in the wilderness took their toll, however. After Sinai even God spoke of the future with a tone of resignation approaching fatalism, like the parent of a drug addict helpless to stop his own child from self-destruction.

Two staged memory lessons were not enough. Despite Moses' exhausted state, God required one more task of him, an odd assignment indeed. Write down a song, God said, and make the Israelites learn it as a witness to history. Laws written on stone and plaster, curses and blessings broadcast from the mountaintops—these sights and sounds will fade away. Make them, every one of them, learn my words by heart. Drill the message inside them.

The song that appears in Deuteronomy 32 sets to music God's own point of view: the story of a parent grieved to the point of desertion. Thus at the birth of their nation, euphoric over the crossing of the Jordan River, the Israelites premiered a kind of national anthem, the strangest national anthem that has ever been sung. It had virtually no words of hope, only doom.

They sang first of the favored times, when God found them in a howling wasteland and treasured them as the apple of his eye. They sang of the awful betrayal to come, when they would forget the God who gave them birth. They sang of the curses that would afflict them, the wasting famine, deadly plague, and arrows slick with blood. With this bittersweet music ringing in their ears, they marched into the Promised Land.

"I have been to the mountain top," said Martin Luther King Jr. in his final speech, making a haunting allusion to Moses. "[God's] allowed me to go up to the mountain, and I've looked over, and I've seen the promised land. I may not get there with you. But I want you to know tonight that we, as a people will get to the promised land. And so I'm happy tonight. . . . Mine eyes have seen the glory of the coming of the Lord." After that speech King returned to his motel room, was hit by an assassin's bullet, and died in a pool of blood.

On the same day that Moses taught the Israelites the melancholy song of their future, he climbed Mount Nebo, squinted against the sun, and gazed in every direction as far as he could see. He had climbed the mountain. He had seen the Promised Land. There at its frontier, Moses died.

Deuteronomy adds this eulogy: "Since then, no prophet has risen in Israel like Moses, whom the Lord knew face to face, who did all those miraculous signs and wonders the Lord sent him to do in Egypt—to Pharaoh and to all his officials and to his whole land. For no one has ever shown the mighty power or performed the awesome deeds that Moses did in the sight of all Israel."

He was their preacher, historian, soldier, prophet, judge, politician, priest. Centuries later another Jewish writer, Elie Wiesel, elaborated on Moses' contribution:

> Moses, the most solitary and most powerful hero in Biblical history. The immensity of his task and the scope of his experience command our admiration, our reverence, our awe. Moses, the man who changed the course of history all by himself; his emergence became the decisive turning point. After him, nothing was the same again.
>
> It is not surprising that he occupies a special place in the Jewish tradition. His passion for social justice, his struggle for national liberation, his triumphs and disappointments, his poetic inspiration, his gifts as a strategist and his organizational genius, his complex relationship with God and His people, his requirements and promises, his condemnations and blessings, his bursts of anger, his silences, his efforts to reconcile the law with compassion, authority with integrity—no individual, ever, anywhere, accomplished so much for so many people in so many different domains. His influence is boundless, it reverberates beyond time. The Law bears his name, the Talmud is but its commentary and Kabbala communicates only its silence.
>
> —*Messengers of God*

After Moses, nothing was the same again. One man came to stand for his people, and with good reason. Adopted by an imperial parent, punished for his rashness, sentenced to wander forty years in the wilderness, forgiven, restored, hand-selected for an impossible task, accompanied by the overwhelming presence of God at every step—Moses' personal history replays, in miniature, the history of his people.

Modern readers, excited by the thrill of the Exodus, pay little attention to the four hundred years of misery that preceded it, or to the abysmal failures in the Sinai and in the Promised Land that succeeded it. Which is why the Bible includes Deuteronomy in the first place, and why optimistic Americans especially ought to pay it more mind.

Others have borrowed parts of Moses' message, but none have quite got it right. Liberationists of all stripes, from Marxists to American slaves to base communities in Latin America, have appropriated the language of Exodus, yet all lack Moses' unstinting realism. They drift into utopian promises of a Promised Land that has never been, and will never be, realized this side of eternity:

> O Canaan, sweet Canaan,
> I am bound for the land of Canaan.

> Gonna lay down my sword and shield,
> Down by the riverside,
> I ain't gonna study war no more.

Often these utopians end up creating a political system more tyrannical than the one they sought liberation from. African colonies drive out the imperialists only to face new crises of tribalism and independence. Small countries escape the dark shadow of the Soviet Union only to disintegrate into civil war. The Old Testament should come with a warning: Don't read Exodus without also reading Deuteronomy. It would save a lot of disillusionment, for politicians and preachers both.

Pietist Christians have also borrowed Moses' language to describe a Victorious Christian Life on the other side of the Jordan River:

> On Jordan's stormy banks I stand,
> And cast a wishful eye

To Canaan's fair and happy land,
Where my possessions lie.

No chilling winds, nor pois'nous breath
Can reach that healthful shore;
Sickness and sorrow, pain and death,
Are felt and feared no more.

Such visions paint Egypt as a dark land of seductive "flesh-pots," and the wilderness as a trial by ordeal necessary to pass through before arriving in the sun-drenched Promised Land at last. The last seven chapters of Deuteronomy should forever disabuse that notion. Life with God is never so easy, so settled, for any of us. Not for the Hebrews then, and not for us living today. The pilgrim must ever progress, uphill, meeting new enemies around every bend.

Moses was the single greatest realist about life with God. A proto-prophet, he gave God's message to the people, never diluting or belying it. A proto-priest, he represented the people to God with passion, conviction, and love. He made no promises of happy endings—his own life had none—yet never did he look back with regret. The luxuries of Egypt and the solitary comfort of a nomad's life had both lost their appeal. He belonged with his people, the whole swarming, cantankerous lot of them, and with his God, the One he had come to know as a friend, face to face.

"The Lord is compassionate and gracious, slow to anger, abounding in love," sang a psalmist years later, quoting words that Moses had first given to his people. That prayer is still prayed every morning and every evening by Jews around the world. God has bound his love in a covenant, so that even though emotions will rise and fall, in the end the love will always prevail.

He will not always accuse,
    nor will he harbor his anger forever....

For as high as the heavens are above the earth,
   so great is his love for those who fear him;
as far as the east is from the west,
   so far has he removed our transgressions from us.
As a father has compassion on his children,
   so the Lord has compassion on those who fear him;
for he knows how we are formed,
   he remembers that we are dust.

Dust, *Hapiru,* "the dusty ones," the old Egyptian slang word for the Hebrews—God remembers that we are dust. As Moses taught so clearly, evil is unpreventable and punishment inevitable. But we have a God who consciously forgets our sins and consciously remembers our frailty. We have a God who travels by our side, who *tabernacles* among us through the vast and dreadful wilderness. We have a God of grace, who loves even the dusty ones—especially the dusty ones.

⁕⁕⁕⁕

There are two postscripts to Moses' sad, eloquent speeches in Deuteronomy. The first involves an event that occurred after Moses' dire predictions about his people had come true. Following Moses' death, the Hebrews crossed the Jordan, conquered Canaan, built cities, grew strong and prosperous, and promptly forgot about God. The nation split into two, invaders came, Jerusalem fell under siege, and the horror scenes that Moses foretold—parents eating their own children—became a matter of historical record. Once again God intervened with miraculous deliverance, giving his people another chance.

Two kings later the child-king Josiah had the nostalgic notion to repair the temple and renew some of the ancient religious practices. God's holy city had sunk to historic lows. The temple featured idols, male shrine prostitutes, and carved horses dedicated to sun worshipers. In a nearby valley, people burned their children in sacrifice to the god Molech. All sacred records had disappeared; the God of Abraham, Isaac, and Jacob—the God of Moses—was a faint memory. While rummaging through the rubble, the high priest found the "Book of the Covenant," which most likely consisted of portions of Deuteronomy.

Second Kings 22–23 tells the dramatic story of what followed: a spiritual house-cleaning and revival that has few precedents in history. The king wept, tore his robe, and ordered that Moses' law be restored in the nation. At the end of this revolution of belief, Josiah called the whole nation together and celebrated the Passover. "Not since the days of the judges who led Israel, nor throughout the days of the kings of Israel and the kings of Judah, had any such Passover been observed." Moses may have never made it to the Promised Land, but his spirit lived on, bringing renewal, hope, and literal salvation to the descendants of those he led to the border.

The second postscript appears in the New Testament. Jesus knew Deuteronomy well: during his own wilderness sojourn, he quoted from it three times to counter Satan's temptations. Later, at a hinge moment in his ministry, Jesus climbed a high mountain to meet with God the Father. As when Moses met with God on the sacred mountain, Jesus' appearance changed too. "There he was transfigured before them. His face shone like the sun; . . . his clothes became dazzling white, whiter than anyone in the world could bleach them."

Peter, James, and John shrank back, dazed by the scene. A voice rumbled from heaven and suddenly, there on the mountaintop before them, stood two giants of Israelite history. At once they recognized Elijah, the fierce, wonder-working prophet whose return every Jew anticipated. Just to the side— it could be no one else—stood Moses, engaged in casual conversation with Jesus.

Peter grew so excited that he clumsily proposed erecting tents to entice the celestial visitors to stick around. Jesus calmed his disciples, then led them down the mountain back to earth. The miracle gave him new energy and boldness to face difficult days ahead.

The scene of Jesus' transfiguration contains a fact often overlooked by Christians, but poignant for any Jew. At that moment of tender mercy, Moses finally realized his life dream. He stood on a mountaintop smack in the middle of the Promised Land. Indeed, God remembers the dusty ones, the meekest and the greatest.

FOUR

Psalms:
Spirituality in Every Key

FOUR

Psalms: Spirituality in Every Key

If the Psalms have been a source of spiritual instruction and consolation for many seekers, they also have filled others with discomfort and bewilderment. There is an untidiness, a turbulence, an undertow of mystery in these ancient prayers.

—JOHN S. MOGABGAB

I have a confession to make. For years I avoided the book of Psalms. I knew that many Christians looked upon it as their favorite biblical book, that the church had incorporated these poems into public worship, and that overtones from the King James Version of Psalms still reverberated beautifully throughout the language. To this day many editions of the New Testament include Psalms as well, as if it represents an indispensable core of our faith. Yet, hard as I tried, I could never get excited about actually reading Psalms.

People around me used the book as a spiritual medicine cabinet—"If you feel depressed, read Psalm 37; if your health fails, try Psalm 121"—an approach that never worked for me. With uncanny consistency I would land on a psalm that aggravated, rather than cured, my problem. Martin Marty judges at least half the psalms to be "wintry" in tone, and when feeling low I would accidentally turn to one of the wintriest and end up frostily depressed. "The length of our days is seventy years—

or eighty, if we have the strength," prayed Moses in one such psalm, "yet their span is but trouble and sorrow."

Concerned about my bad attitude, I tried an experiment one summer. I was scheduled to spend the month of June in Breckenridge, Colorado, a postcard-perfect town situated almost two miles high in the Rocky Mountains. I decided to rise early each morning, drive a few miles outside town to some pristine wilderness setting, and there read ten psalms in a row. Surely, I thought, mountain sunrises and the magnificent backdrop for my meditations would melt the block that had always kept me from reading Psalms.

Each day I listened to birds make their wake-up announcements and watched the sun turn snowcaps pink, then orange, then blazing white. One morning I sat beside a pond as a family of beavers made repairs to an elaborate series of dams. Another time, a ten-point deer wandered directly in front of me and drank from a mountain stream. I would like to report that this experiment transformed my attitude toward Psalms. I came away with stunning visual memories and a renewed spirit of worship, but, alas, reading the book itself frustrated, rather than inspired, me.

More than anything, I felt confused while reading Psalms, especially because I had committed to ten in a row. Individual psalms seemed to contradict each other violently: psalms of bleak despair abutted psalms of soaring joy, as if the scribes had arranged them with a mockingly Hegelian sense of humor. The first day, for example, my spirits soared as I read Psalm 8:

> When I consider your heavens,
>   the work of your fingers,
> the moon and the stars,
>   which you have set in place,
> what is man that you are mindful of him,
>   the son of man that you care for him?

The moon, silvery bright against an azure sky, still hung suspended above a 14,000-foot peak. The night before, the Milky

Way had stretched across the sky like a highway of lights. Amid the grandeur and huge expanse of Alpine scenery, I found myself marveling along with the psalmist at our favored human role in the creation drama.

The next psalm continued in the same spirit, praising God for his eternal reign, his fairness in judging the world, his mercy to the oppressed, his trustworthiness. Then suddenly with Psalm 10 the mood abruptly shifted. Just before ending my meditations I encountered these jarring words:

> Why, O Lord, do you stand far off?
> Why do you hide yourself in times of trouble?

From these doubts, the psalmist dives into a vicious description of "the wicked man" and demands that God "break the arm of the wicked and evil man." So much for my state of serenity and worship. To complicate matters, I learned from a study Bible that Psalms 9 and 10 were possibly written as one psalm, the contrary moods tugging against each other within the very same poem.

Every day I faced this same pattern of glaring contradictions. Instead of beginning the day with devotional peace, I felt swept along on an emotional roller-coaster, plummeting to the depths of despair and soaring to heights of praise all in the same one-hour period. That, combined with the thin mountain air and a possible overdose of coffee, left me feeling slightly buzzed for the remainder of the day.

After a week of this practice, I ran into yet another problem. The psalms started to sound boring and repetitive. Why, I wondered, did the Bible need 150 psalms? Wouldn't fifteen suffice to cover the basic content? I struggled through my ten psalms every day but left Breckenridge with an even worse attitude toward Psalms. My experiment had failed. In guilt-ridden evangelical fashion, I blamed myself, not the Bible, for the failure.

Back in the flatland of Illinois, I tried a new approach, studying the book systematically. I learned to appreciate the poetic craftsmanship involved in Hebrew parallelism and in the acrostic form. I learned to differentiate the types of psalms: imprecatory psalms, psalms of lament, psalms of ascent, royal psalms, thank-offering psalms. I learned the various ways of explaining the problem psalms. After acquiring all this knowledge, I read the psalms with a heightened sense of comprehension but with no heightened sense of enjoyment. As a result, for years I simply avoided the book. You can find a psalm that says anything, I reasoned. Matter of fact, you can find a dozen psalms that say the very same thing. Why bother with them?

Reading Over Someone's Shoulder

I now realize how impoverished was that view. In my fixation with the details of the psalms—their categories, interpretive meaning, logical consistency, poetic form—I had missed the main point, which is that the book of Psalms comprises a sampling of spiritual journals, much like personal letters to God. I had lacked a lens through which to view the book. I must read them as an "over-the-shoulder" reader since the intended audience was not other people, but God. Even the psalms for public use were designed as corporate prayers: for them too God represented the primary audience.

I suppose I had been trying subconsciously to fit the psalms into the scriptural grid established by the apostle Paul. These, however, are not pronouncements from on high, delivered with full apostolic authority, on matters of faith and practice. They are personal prayers in the form of poetry, written by a variety of people—peasants, kings, professional musicians, rank amateurs—in wildly fluctuating moods. Job and Deuteronomy offer the extraordinary cases of two renowned, righteous men trying to relate to God through difficult times. Psalms gives examples of "ordinary" people struggling mightily to align what they believe about God with what they actually experience. Sometimes the authors are vindictive, sometimes self-righteous, sometimes paranoid, sometimes petty.

Do not misunderstand me: I do not believe Psalms to be any less valuable, or less inspired, than Paul's letters or the Gospels. Nevertheless, the psalms do use an inherently different approach, not so much representing God to the people as the people representing themselves to God. Yes, Psalms belongs as part of God's Word, but in the same way Job or Ecclesiastes belongs. We read the speeches of Job's friends—accurate records of misguided thinking—in a different way than we read the Sermon on the Mount. "The psalms do not theologize," writes Kathleen Norris in *The Cloister Walk*, "One reason for this is that the psalms are poetry, and poetry's function is not to explain but to offer images and stories that resonate with our lives."

Understanding this distinction changed the way I read Psalms. Formerly, I had approached the book as a graduate student might approach a textbook: I skimmed the poetry in search of CORRECT AND IMPORTANT CONCEPTS to be noted and neatly classified. Psalms resists such systematization and will, I think, drive mad anyone who tries to wrest from it a rigid organizational schema. I learned to approach the book in a very different way.

Let me illustrate. My father died when I was thirteen months old. I have no conscious memories of him and very few mementos from his brief life on earth. I cherish a few fuzzy photos of him holding a fat baby with blond curls—me—as well as a crude statue he had carved as a boy and a handful of books from his library, among them a worn, black Scofield Reference Bible. Even now I can glean something of my father's relationship with God by reading the notes in the margins of that Bible, for he used the white space to record a kind of spiritual journal. He never had me in mind when he wrote those notes, for I did not yet exist. Yet, years later I can be moved, challenged, and convicted as I read about his own relationship with God.

The psalms are more formal than my father's scribbled notes, of course. They came out of a common context, God's covenant relationship with Israel, and the authors expressed themselves in beautiful, sometimes highly structured poetry. Now, as I read them, I begin by trying to project myself back into the minds of those authors—just as I project myself back into the mind of my father who wrote those fragmentary notes. *Could I pray these prayers?* I ask myself. *Have I felt this peculiar anguish? This outburst of praise?* Then I proceed to think through situations in which I might pray the psalm in front of me. Facing temptation, celebrating a success, harboring a grudge, suffering an injustice—under what circumstances would this psalm best apply in my life?

Any one of the psalms, wrenched from the rest of the book, may mislead. In a thoughtful reflection on Psalm 91 published in *Christianity Today*, author Neal Plantinga considers its beautiful image of God's protection, "He will cover you with his feathers, and under his wings you will find refuge.... If you make the Most High your dwelling—even the Lord, who is my refuge—then no harm will befall you...." Oh? Plantinga muses. What about Christians arrested by the Nazis in World War II, or by hostile Muslim governments today? How must that psalm sound as they read it on the eve of execution? The psalms' sweeping promises of safety seem patently untrue.

Plantinga recalls that Satan himself quoted from this psalm, jerking it out of context, in an attempt to get Jesus to jump from a high place. Jesus rebuked him with another passage of Scripture. Says Plantinga,

> What Psalm 91 does is express *one*—one of the loveliest, one of the most treasured—but just *one* of the moods of faith. It's a mood of exuberant confidence in the shelter-

ing providence of God. Probably the psalmist has been protected by God in some dangerous incident, and he is celebrating.

On other days, and in other moods—in other and darker seasons of his life—this same psalmist might have called to God out of despair and a sense of abandonment. [Here Plantinga cites Jesus' cry of Psalm 22 from the cross.]

Psalm 91 gives us only part of the picture and only one of the moods of faith. With a kind of quiet amazement, the psalmist bears witness that under the wings of God good things happen to bad people. You need another psalm or two to fill in the picture, to cry out that under those same wings bad things sometimes happen to good people.

Psalms, located in the exact center of the Bible, gives us a comprehensive record of life with God through individually fashioned accounts of how the spiritual life works. I come to the psalms not primarily as a student wanting to acquire knowledge, but rather as a fellow pilgrim wanting to acquire relationship. The first and greatest commandment is to love the Lord our God with all our hearts and all our souls and all our minds. More than any other book in the Bible, Psalms reveals what a heartfelt, soul-starved, single-minded relationship with God looks like.

Messy and Disordered, like Life

Poetry works its magic subtly. In modern times, at least, we rarely seek out poetry for didactic purposes, to learn something. We turn to it because the poet's shaping of words and images gives us pleasure and moves our emotions. Yet if the poet succeeds, we may gain something greater than knowledge: a transformed vision. That is the magic the psalms have ultimately worked upon me. They have transformed my spiritual vision and my understanding of relationship with God.

At a basic level, the psalms help me reconcile what I believe about life with what I actually encounter in life. When I was a child, I learned this mealtime prayer: "God is great. God is good. Let us thank him for this food." Its cadence has a certain incantatory charm, and indeed the prayer sounds as if it could have come from Psalms. What could be simpler: two foundational assertions of theology and a spirit of thanksgiving, all conveniently expressed in one-syllable words.

Nevertheless, I must tell you that praying this simple prayer with honesty and conviction has been an Abrahamic trial of faith. God is great? Why don't we see more conspicuous evidence? Why are the scientists, who make their living studying the wonders of natural creation, less likely than an illiterate peasant to attribute those wonders to God? Why has our century been so cursed by a succession of anti-god tyrants: Stalin, Hitler, Idi Amin, Pol Pot? Why have more Christians died for their faith in this century than in all others combined?

God is good? Why did my father, a young man with unlimited potential as a missionary, die before reaching the age of thirty? Why did all those Jews and Christians die unjustly in the Holocaust? Why is the most religious portion of our population, inner-city African-Americans, the most poverty-stricken and hopeless?

Thank him for this food? I kept up that practice even through smart-alecky days of adolescence, when I attributed more credit to the abundance of American rivers and the wizardry of farmers. What of the Christians in Sudan or Mozambique, though? How can they thank God while dying for want of food?

If reading the last three paragraphs has made you slightly uncomfortable, perhaps you should read Psalms again. It contains the anguished journals of people who want to believe in a loving, gracious, faithful God while the world keeps falling apart around them.

The psalmists often expressed variations on the themes I have mentioned. Why should those nasty Amalekites, Hittites, Philistines, and Canaanites, not to mention the juggernaut empires of Assyria, Babylon, and Persia, take turns crushing *God's chosen people?* Why should David, anointed by God to be king, spend a decade hiding out in caves and dodging the spears of Saul, whom God had ordered to step down? How can God's people feel thankful when there seems so little to feel thankful about?

Many psalms show their authors fiercely struggling with such questions. Sometimes the poets find a way to align the emotions of faith with the doctrines of faith in the very course of writing the psalm. Like Moses giving the speeches of Deuteronomy, they review God's involvement in Israel's history, forcing themselves to remember the good times.

> Look to the Lord and his strength;
>   seek his face always.
> Remember the wonders he has done,
>   his miracles, and the judgments he pronounced.
>   (105:4–5)

Psalm 62 boldly, without explanation, insists on two facts that Job could never put together: "that you, O God, are strong, and that you, O Lord, are loving." Sometimes, however, the poets cannot make sense of what they see, and the psalmists end up sounding exactly like Job:

> I am worn out calling for help;
>   my throat is parched.
> My eyes fail,
>   looking for my God. (69:3)

At this point the seemingly random ordering of the 150 psalms comes into play, for the seesaw cycle of intimacy and abandonment is, in fact, what most people experience in their relationship with God.

The most startling juxtaposition of psalms occurs early on. Psalm 23, that shepherd song of sweeping promise and consummate comfort, follows on the heels of Psalm 22, which opens with the words Jesus cried from the cross, "My God, my God, why have you forsaken me?" The two psalms, both attributed to David, could hardly form a more glaring contrast. True, David does find some sort of resolution in Psalm 22, by looking ahead to a future time when God will rule over the nations and the poor will eat their fill. But he makes clear how he feels at the moment of writing: "I cry out by day, but you do not answer.... I am a worm and not a man.... Roaring lions tearing their prey open their mouths wide against me.... all my bones are out of joint.... my tongue sticks to the roof of my mouth." Such sentiments seem from another planet when you turn the page and read, "The Lord is my shepherd, I shall not be in want.... Surely goodness and love will follow me all the days of my life."

A similar discord marks Psalms 102 and 103. The first (subtitled "A prayer of an afflicted man. When he is faint and pours out his lament before the Lord.") eloquently expresses the despair of an aging, weakened man who feels abandoned by all friends and by God. It reads like a catalog of pain scratched out by a hospital patient in a febrile state. The next psalm, however, a majestic hymn of praise, includes not one note in the minor key.

I doubt many pastors choose to preach on either pairing of those consecutive psalms—one or the other, maybe, but not both. I have learned to appreciate Psalms precisely because it does encompass both points of view, often adjoined with no calming transition. "Praise the Lord, O my soul, and forget not his benefits," says Psalm 103. The author of its nearest neighbor is desperately trying to recall God's benefits, no easy task in his condition, bones burning like glowing embers, on a diet of ashes and tears.

I, for one, am glad my Bible includes both kinds of psalms. A time may come when I feel like the author of Psalm 22 or 102, and when that time comes I will take comfort in the fact that spiritual giants—most notably, Jesus himself—have felt that way too. And although I may groan and cry out and resist the trial that entangles me in its net, I will also try to recall the tranquil message of Psalms 23 and 103. By itself, Psalm 23 leads to an easy-answer faith; by itself Psalm 22 leads to spiritual despair; together, the two offer a bracing mixture of realism and hope.

I have come to see these psalms as calling for different kinds of faith. Psalm 23 models childlike faith, and Psalm 22 models fidelity, a deeper, more mysterious kind of faith. Life with God may include both. We may experience times of unusual closeness, when prayers are answered in an obvious way and God seems intimate and caring. We may also experience dark times, when God stays silent, when nothing works according to formula and all the Bible's promises seem glaringly false. Fidelity involves learning to trust that, out beyond the perimeter of darkness, God still reigns and has not abandoned us, no matter how it may appear.

The 150 psalms are as difficult, disordered, and messy as life itself, a fact that can bring unexpected comfort. Kathleen Norris describes in *The Cloister Walk* how she has learned to bring the psalms into her current situation by "praying the news":

> Psalm 74's lament on the violation of sacred space— "Every cave in the land is a place where violence has made its home"—has become for me a prayer for the victims and perpetrators of domestic violence. Watching television footage of the Los Angeles riots of early 1992 gave me a new context for the words of Psalm 55 that I encountered the next morning in the monastic choir: "I see nothing but violence and strife in the city." Hearing Psalm 79 ("They have poured out blood like water in Jerusalem / there is no one left to bury the dead") as I

read of civil war in the Balkans forces me to reflect on the evil that tribalism and violence, often justified by religion, continue to inflict on our world.

But the relentless realism of the psalms is not depressing in the way that television news can be, although many of the same events are reported: massacres, injustices to those who have no one to defend them, people tried in public by malicious tongues. As a book of praises, meant to be sung, the Psalter contains a hope that "human interest" stories tacked onto the end of a news broadcast cannot provide. The psalms mirror our world but do not allow us to become voyeurs. In a nation unwilling to look at its own violence, they force us to recognize our part in it. They make us re-examine our values.

Here is what Psalms can do for a person in distress. In 1977, at the height of the Cold War, Anatoly Shcharansky, a brilliant young mathematician and chess player, was arrested by the KGB for his repeated attempts to emigrate to Israel. He spent thirteen years inside the Soviet Gulag. From morning to evening Shcharansky read and studied all 150 psalms (in Hebrew). "What does this give me?" he asked in a letter: "Gradually, my feeling of great loss and sorrow changes to one of bright hopes."

Shcharansky so cherished his book of Psalms, in fact, that when guards took it away from him, he lay in the snow, refusing to move, until they returned it. During those thirteen years, his wife traveled around the world campaigning for his release. Accepting an honorary degree on his behalf, she told the university audience, "In a lonely cell in Chistopol prison, locked alone with the Psalms of David, Anatoly found expression for his innermost feelings in the outpourings of the King of Israel thousands of years ago."

Soul Therapy

The psalms give me a model of spiritual therapy. I once wrote a book titled *Disappointment with God*, and my publishers initially worried over the title, proposing instead *Overcoming Disappointment with God.* It seemed faintly heretical to introduce a book with a negative title into Christian bookstores filled with books on the marvelous Christian life. In the process of writing the book, however, I found that the Bible includes detailed accounts of people sorely disappointed with God—to put it mildly. Not only Job and Moses have it out with God; so do Habakkuk, Jeremiah, and many of the unnamed psalmists. Some psalms merit titles like "Furious with God," "Betrayed by God," "Abandoned by God," "In Despair about God."

Consider a few lines from Psalm 89:

How long, O Lord? Will you hide yourself forever?
How long will your wrath burn like fire? ...
For what futility you have created all men!

Or these sentiments from Psalm 88:

Why, O Lord, do you reject me
and hide your face from me? ...
the darkness is my closest friend.

It may seem strange for sacred writings to include such scenes of spiritual failure, but actually their inclusion reflects an important principle of therapy. A marriage therapist will often warn new clients, "Your relationship may get worse before it gets better." Grudges and resentments that have been buried for years may resurface. Misunderstandings must be nakedly exposed before true understanding can begin to flourish. Indeed, the psalms, like psychoanalysis, may help uncover neurotic elements in us.

Kathleen Norris writes of a Catholic sister who counsels troubled women—displaced homemakers, abused wives, women returning to college after years away—and finds that Psalms offers a helpful pattern of expressing rage that the church often tries to repress. "Bear it up; keep smiling; suffering makes you strong," say some spiritual advisors—but not the psalmists. They do not rationalize anger away or give abstract advice about pain; rather, they express emotions vividly and loudly, directing their feelings primarily at God.

The 150 psalms present a mosaic of spiritual therapy in process. Doubt, paranoia, giddiness, meanness, delight, hatred, joy, praise, vengefulness, betrayal—you can find it all in Psalms. Such strewing of emotions, which I once saw as hopeless disarray, I now see as a sign of health. From Psalms I have learned that I can rightfully bring to God *whatever* I feel about him. I need not paper over my failures and try to clean up my own rottenness; far better to bring those weaknesses to God, who alone has the power to heal.

No psalm demonstrates healing power better than Psalm 51, credited to David after his sordid affair with Bathsheba (see 2 Samuel 11 and 12). Even though he had committed murder and adultery, David recognized that in the final analysis, "Against you [God], you only have I sinned." Although he had nothing to offer God but a broken spirit and a contrite heart, that very admission led him down the path toward healing. David confessed, in tears and grief, and the psalm became a public guide for others' confession.

Walter Brueggemann has coined the term "psalms of disorientation" to describe those psalms that express confusion, confession, and doubt. Typically, the writer begins by begging God to rescue him from his desperate straits. He may weave poetic images of how he has been wronged, appeal to God's sense of justice, even taunt God: "What good can I do you when I'm dead? How can I praise you then?" The very act of venting these feelings allows the author to attain a better perspective. He reflects on better times, remembers answered prayers of the past, concedes favors that he may have overlooked. By the end of the psalm, he moves toward praise and thanksgiving. He feels heard and cleansed. The psalm, or prayer, works out the transformation.

Psalm 71 gives an example of how this "spiritual reality therapy" may work. The stanzas move from urgent pleas for God's help to tentative declarations of faith to new fears for the future. By the end, the poet is praising God for his faithfulness. Forced memory, of God's miracles for Israel and God's past intimacy in his own life, has put to rest, for the present, some of the poet's fundamental doubts. Many psalms convey this spirit of "Lord, I believe, help my unbelief," a way of talking oneself into faith when emotions are wavering.

The odd mixture of psalms of cursing, psalms of praise, and psalms of confession no longer jars me as it once did. Instead, I am continually amazed by the spiritual wholeness of the Hebrew poets, who sought to include God in every area of life by bringing to God every emotion experienced in daily activity. One need not "dress up" or "put on a face" to meet God. There are no walled-off areas; God can be trusted with reality.

For the Hebrew poets, God represented a reality more solid than their own whipsaw emotions or the checkered history of their people. They wrestled with God over every facet of their lives, and in the end it was the very act of wrestling that proved their faith.

I have a friend, Harold Fickett, who retires for days at a time to a nearby monastery. Many monastic orders recite the psalms aloud morning, noon, and evening. It takes them several weeks to go through the entire cycle, at which point they begin again with Psalm 1.* Harold tells me that sometimes his voice is describing "coming into the Lord's gates with thanksgiving" while his mind is replaying some offensive remark he

---

*Until recently every Roman Catholic priest who said the Divine Office from his breviary went through all the psalms once a week. The Anglican liturgy takes a month to make it through all 150. Historian Paul Johnson mentions Psalms as one of the great unifiers of Christian history: Benedictines and Puritans, Luther and Xavier, Wesley and Newman and Calvin all loved and continually recited the psalms.

heard yesterday or wondering when the fog will lift from San Francisco Bay. Day by day he picks up the rhythm of the psalms. Not all apply to his current spiritual state. Gradually, though, he enters into the reality conveyed in the psalms, rather than trying to force them into his own mundane world.

Reflecting on his time with the monks, Harold wrote that

> the Psalms supply me with the words that I need and sometimes want to say to my God. Words that celebrate his reality: "The heavens declare the glory of God." Words that confess his action in my life: "You have turned my mourning into dancing." Words that express my utter dependence: "In my mother's womb, you formed me." Words that convey my hoped-for intimacy: "This one thing I desire, that I might dwell in the house of the Lord forever." The Psalms tutor my soul in my love for God.

Praise Chords

On a different note, the psalms also teach how to adore and how to praise, activities that Americans perform with notorious awkwardness. We have not the tradition of British subjects, who curtsy to the queen and never interrupt her. We feel more comfortable roasting politicians in comedy revues than bowing to them.

Frankly, the whole notion of God asking us to sit around saying nice things about him can seem rather alien. Why does God need our praise anyway? Somerset Maugham had a devout relative who went through the *Book of Common Prayer* and crossed out everything on praise. People are uncomfortable with compliments to their face, he reasoned, so surely God would not want them either. Similarly, C. S. Lewis remarked in his *Reflections on the Psalms*, "I don't want my dog to bark approval of my books." Why would God desire praise?

Lewis went on to suggest that we might best imagine praise by thinking of our instinctive response to a great work of art or a symphony or extraordinary beauty in any form. The natural response is, first, to pause and enjoy the surpassing beauty— almost as if kneeling before it—and then to announce it to others. Such a response of shared enjoyment works on many levels: "A gray whale swam right up to our boat off California—I could have touched her!" "Oh, I wish you could be here to see the snow fall. It makes everything so beautiful." "Weren't the Broncos devastating yesterday?"

I see this kind of praise, approaching worship, whenever I attend a professional sporting event. I was fortunate enough to live in Chicago during Michael Jordan's peak years, and several times I attended Chicago Bulls games. Hours before the game, despite the freezing Chicago weather, fans would line the team parking lot for a glimpse of the superstar. When his Blazer turned in, they would scream, jump up and down, call out his name, beg for an autograph, a wave, a touch, any token of connection with The Great One. How odd that a culture that readily gives adulation to Michael Jordan, or even to naughty role models such as Dennis Rodman or Madonna, finds praise to God so alien.

Praise takes the instinctive response of shared enjoyment (ever try keeping a great joke to yourself, or the fact that you just got engaged?) and raises it a few notches. "Tell me the old, old story of unseen things above," says one old gospel song, and praise is partly that. Just as sports fans or Army veterans or high school classmates love to recount the same stories over and over again, praise offers that same nostalgic opportunity.

Flannery O'Connor once wrote an essay about her peacocks and the reactions they would get as they unfurled their feathers to present "a galaxy of gazing, haloed suns." One truck driver yelled, "Get a load of that!" and braked to a halt. Most people would fall silent. Her favorite response came from an old black woman who simply cried, "Amen! Amen!" That woman understood praise.

In praise, the creature happily acknowledges that everything good and true and beautiful in the universe comes from the Creator. The affirmation works on us as well as on God, by reminding us of our proper position before God. To develop praise, I have found, it helps to hang around children. They have no problem bursting out in spontaneous praise when something impresses them, perhaps because they have no pretension to rise above their assigned state—as children.

Authors of the psalms, especially David, had an advantage in praise because of their closer tie to the natural world. David began life outdoors as a shepherd, then spent years hiding from Saul in the rocky terrain of Israel. Not surprisingly, a great love, even reverence, for the natural world shines through many of his poems. Psalms presents a world that fits together as a whole, with everything upheld by a personal God watching over it.

This message, above all, leaped out at me during my frustrating attempts to read the psalms in Colorado. I could not fit together all the contradictory messages I was reading, but the magnificent wilderness setting at least affirmed the message of God's grandeur, his *worthiness*. Wilderness brings us down a level, reminding us of something we'd prefer to forget: our creatureliness. It announces to our senses the splendor of an invisible, untamable God. How could I not offer praise to the One who dreamed up porcupines and elk, who splashed brightgreen aspen trees across hillsides of gray rock, who transforms that same landscape into a new work of art with every blizzard?

According to the psalms, praise need not be sober and reflective. The psalmists praised God with sensuous abandon, and as a result their worship services may well have resembled a modern pep rally more than a sedate symphony concert. "Sing for joy! Shout aloud!" they command. Musical instruments in those days included cymbals, tambourines, trumpets, rams' horns, harps, and lyres. Sometimes dancing erupted. The world, in the psalmist's imagination, cannot contain the delight God inspires. A new song breaks out: "Shout for joy to the Lord, all the earth, burst into jubilant song" (98:4). Nature itself joins in: "Let the rivers clap their hands, let the mountains sing together for joy" (98:8).

The psalms wonderfully solve the problem of a praise-deficient culture by providing the necessary words. We merely need to enter into those words, letting the content of the psalms realign our inner attitudes. Dietrich Bonhoeffer suggests that the psalms are God's language course. Just as infants learn the mother tongue from their parents, Christians can learn the language of prayer from Psalms.

"Worship," says Eugene Peterson,

> is the strategy by which we interrupt our preoccupation with ourselves and attend to the presence of God. Worship is the time and place that we assign for deliberate attentiveness to God—not because he's confined to time and place but because our self-importance is so insidiously relentless that if we don't deliberately interrupt ourselves regularly, we have no chance of attending to him at all at other times and in other places.
>
> —*Leap Over a Wall*

When the ancient Hebrews encountered something beautiful or majestic, their natural response was not to contemplate the scene or to analyze it, but rather to praise God for it and maybe write a poem. Their fingers itched for the harp; their vocal cords longed for the hymn. Praise, for them, was joy expressing itself in song and speech, an "inner health made audible," in C. S. Lewis's phrase. Because of them, we too can enter into that health.

Of all the creatures both in sea and land
Only to Man thou hast made known thy ways,

And put the pen alone into his hand,
And made him Secretary of thy praise.

—George Herbert

Realignment

Eugene Peterson, recent translator of Psalms, admits that only a minority focus on praise and thanksgiving; perhaps as many as seventy percent take the form of laments. These two categories, says Peterson, correspond to the two large conditions in which we find ourselves: distress and well-being. I have never conducted a survey, but I have a hunch that the average Christian bookstore reverses the proportions: at least seventy percent of the books, plaques, and gift items speak to our well-being, while a much smaller percentage speak to our distress.

King David specifically ordered that his people be taught how to lament (2 Samuel 1:18). The lament in Psalms has little in common with whining or complaining. We whine about things we have little control over; we lament what we believe ought to be changed. Like Job, the psalmists clung to a belief in God's ultimate goodness, no matter how things appeared at the present, and cried out for justice. They lamented that God's will was not being done on earth as it was in Heaven; the resulting poetry helped realign their eternal beliefs with their daily experience.

Dan Allender, a Christian counselor, asks,

> To whom do you vocalize the most intense, irrational—meaning inchoate, inarticulate—anger? Would you do so with someone who could fire you or cast you out of a cherished position or relationship? Not likely. You don't trust them—you don't believe they would endure the depths of your disappointment, confusion. . . . The person who hears your lament and far more bears your lament against them, paradoxically, is someone you

deeply, wildly trust. . . . The language of lament is oddly the shadow side of faith.

Because many psalms were written by Israel's leaders, the book offers a unique behind-the-scenes view of a people's emotional history. I know of no comparable collection of private reactions to an ancient history. In Psalms we can read what a king prayed after committing adultery and murder, and what he prayed after escaping an assassination attempt, and after losing a crucial battle, and after dedicating a new capital city to God.

I once did an exercise to try to better understand David. The same king that taught his people to lament also gave them an incomparable hymn of public confession and penned numerous magnificent songs of praise. David was as obviously flawed as anyone in the Old Testament, and yet somehow he became known as "a man after God's own heart." John Calvin wrote, "David is like a mirror, in which God sets before us the continued course of his grace." What was David's spiritual secret?

The seventy-three psalms attributed to David offer a window into his soul, especially since some of them have introductory comments revealing the actual circumstances in which they were written. I decided to read from David's spiritual diary of psalms first and then, from the evidence of that "inner" record, try to imagine what "outer" events prompted such words. Afterward I turned to the historical account in the books of Samuel and compared my inventions with what had actually taken place.

In Psalm 56 (which includes the famous words, "In God I trust") David gratefully credits God for delivering his soul from death and his feet from stumbling. As I read the psalm, it sounded to me as if God had miraculously intervened and rescued David from some predicament. What actually happened? I turned to 1 Samuel 21 and read the story of a scared prisoner who drooled spittle and flung himself about like a madman in a desperate attempt to save his own neck. There was no miracle, so far as I could see, just a canny renegade with strong survival instincts. Perhaps David cried out to God in desperation, and in that moment the idea of faking insanity came to mind—if so, he gave God all the credit and saved none for himself. Surprisingly, David even used the acrostic form to express his thoughts, beginning each verse with the next letter of the Hebrew alphabet; he intended it as a formal, serious reflection on what happened.

Next, I read Psalm 59: "O my Strength, I sing praise to you; you, O God, are my fortress, my loving God." Once again it seemed from the psalm that God had intervened to save David's life. Yet in 1 Samuel 19, the corresponding passage, I read of a chase scene: David sneaked out through a window while his wife diverted the pursuers by wrapping a statue in goat's hair. Once more, David's psalm gave God all the credit for what looked like human ingenuity.

Psalm 57 introduces a new tone, of weakness and trembling. David's faith must have been wavering when he wrote that psalm, I surmised. Wrong again. When I looked up the historical account in 1 Samuel 24, I found one of the most extraordinary displays of defiant courage in all of history.

Psalm 18 gives a summary of David's entire military career. Written when he was undisputed king at last, it recalls in incandescent detail the many miracles of deliverance from God. If you read just that psalm, and not the background history, you would think David lived a charmed and sheltered life. The psalm tells nothing of the years on the run, the all-night battles, the chase scenes, and the wily escape plots that fill the pages of 1 and 2 Samuel.

In short, if you read the psalms attributed to David and then try to envision his life, you will fail miserably. You might imagine a pious, other-worldly hermit or a timid, neurotic soul favored by God, but never a giant of strength and valor. What can explain the disparity between the two biblical records of David's inward and outward journeys?

We all experience both an inner life and an outer life simultaneously. If I attend the same event as you (say, a party), I will take home similar "outer" facts about what happened and who was there but a wholly different "inner" point of view. My memory will dwell on what impression I made. Was I witty or charming? Did I offend someone or embarrass myself? Did I look good to others? Most likely, you will ask the same questions, but about yourself.

David seemed to view life differently. His exploits—killing wild animals bare-handed, felling Goliath, surviving Saul's onslaughts, routing the Philistines—surely earned him a starring role. Nonetheless, as he reflected on those events and wrote poems about them, he found a way to make Jehovah, God of Israel, the one on center stage. Whatever the phrase "practicing the presence of God" means, David experienced it. Whether he expressed that presence in lofty poems of praise or in an earthy harangue, in either case he intentionally involved God in the details of his life.

David had confidence that he mattered to God. After one narrow escape he wrote, "[God] rescued me because he delighted in me" (Psalm 18:19). When David felt betrayed by God, he let God know: it was he, after all, who first said the words, "My God, my God, why have you forsaken me?" He called God into account, insisting that God keep up his end of their special relationship.

Throughout his life David believed, truly believed, that the spiritual world, though invisible to him, was every bit as real as the "natural" world of swords and spears and caves and thrones. His psalms form a record of a conscious effort to reorient his own daily life to the reality of that supernatural world beyond him. Now, centuries later, we can use those very same prayers as steps of faith, a path to lead us from an obsession with ourselves to the actual presence of our God.

That process of "letting God in" on every detail of life is one I need to learn from. In the busy, industrialized modern world, we tend to compartmentalize our lives. We fill our days with activities—getting the car repaired, taking vacations, going to work, mowing the lawn, chauffeuring the kids—and then try to carve out some time for "spiritual" activities such as church, small groups, personal devotions. I see none of that separation in Psalms.

Somehow, David and the other poets managed to make God the gravitational center of their lives so that everything related to God. To them, worship was the central activity in life, not something to get over in order to resume other activity. As C. S. Lewis has said, ideally being a practicing Christian "means that every single act and feeling, every experience, whether pleasant or unpleasant, must be referred to God."

I am learning this daily process of reorientation, and Psalms has become for me a step in the process of recognizing God's true place at the gravitational center. I am trying to make the prayers first prayed by the Hebrew poets authentically my prayers. The New Testament writers did this, quoting Psalms more than any other book. The Son of God on earth did likewise, relying on them as the language of relationship between a human being and God.

I am sure that making the psalms my own prayers will require a lifelong commitment. I sense in them an urgency, a desire and hunger for God that makes my own look anemic by contrast. The psalmists panted for God with their tongues hanging out, as an exhausted deer pants for water. They lay awake at night dreaming of "the fair beauty of the Lord." They would rather spend one day in God's presence than a thousand years elsewhere. It was the advanced school of faith these poets were enrolled in, and often I feel more like a kindergartner. Now that I've started to read Psalms again, maybe some of it will rub off.

Postscript

Problem Psalms

You don't have to read far in Psalms before encountering some troubling passages, furious outbursts hidden like landmines in the midst of soothing pastoral poetry. Some seem on the level of "I hope you get hit by a truck!" schoolyard epithets. "Imprecatory psalms" these are called, or sometimes "vindictive psalms," or, more bluntly, "cursing psalms" because of the curses they rain down on opponents.

The cursing psalms present a major obstacle to most readers. "How in the world can we read, let alone pray, these angry and often violent poems from an ancient warrior culture?" asks Kathleen Norris. "At a glance, they seem overwhelmingly patriarchal, ill-tempered, moralistic, vengeful, and often seem to reflect precisely what is wrong with our world."

Why are such outbursts lurking in the midst of sacred scriptures? Readers have proposed various explanations.

1. The cursing psalms express an appropriate "righteous anger" over evil.

The late Professor Allan Bloom, author of *The Closing of The American Mind*, told about asking his undergraduate class at the University of Chicago to identify an evil person. Not one student could do so. "Evil" simply did not exist as a category in their minds. The inability to recognize and identify evil, said Bloom, is a perilous sign in our society.

I have received great help on this issue from my wife, Janet, who for several years worked near an inner-city housing project. She saw pervasive evil every day: the gangs who sniped at sidewalk pedestrians with automatic rifles, the policemen who roughed up innocent people because of skin color, the thieves who knocked down senior citizens outside the currency exchange where they cashed their Social Security checks.

One evening Janet came home boiling with anger. A janitor was tyrannizing the residents of one senior citizens' building. He would use his master key to enter widows' apartments, then beat them up and steal their money. Everyone knew the culprit, but because he wore a mask and could not be positively identified, the city housing authority was stalling on his transfer or dismissal. If Allan Bloom had asked my wife to describe an evil person that day, he would have gotten a graphic description.

It was precisely that kind of structural evil—corrupt judges, slave owners, robbers, oppressors of the poor, racists, terrorists—that the psalmists were responding to. Psalm 109 calls down curses on a man who "hounded to death the poor and the needy and the brokenhearted. He loved to pronounce a curse—may it come on him."

In reading the cursing psalms, think of the testimony from victims' families that sometimes gets air play on television news. The father of a daughter killed by a drunk driver stands before the court and, physically shaking, tells of the wound that will never be healed. Or think of the Goldman family's statements against O. J. Simpson during the civil trial against him. In his reflections on Psalms, Dietrich Bonhoeffer had no trouble understanding the sentiments behind the cursing psalms; they precisely expressed the anguish of the entire Christian community living under Nazi rule.

The "righteous anger" explanation may illuminate the motives behind the cursing psalms, but it does not remove all the problems they present. Although furious, Janet did not stalk around the house muttering threats like, "May his children be wandering beggars; may they be driven from their ruined homes" (109:10), or, "Happy is he ... who seizes your infants and dashes them against the rocks" (137:9).

2. The cursing psalms express a spiritual immaturity corrected by the New Testament.

C. S. Lewis, genuinely chagrined by the cursing psalms, discussed this approach in his book *Reflections on the Psalms*. He contrasted the psalmists' spirit of vengefulness with another spirit—"Love your enemies"; "Forgive them for they know not what they do"—exemplified in the New Testament. "The reaction of the Psalmists to injury, though profoundly natural, is profoundly wrong," Lewis concluded. He used words like "diabolical," "contemptible," "ferocious," "barbaric," and "self-pitying" to describe these sentiments.

Observing nothing comparable to the psalmists' vindictive spirit in pagan literature, Lewis developed a rather complicated argument related to the election of the Jews. "Of all bad men religious bad men are the worst," he said. The Jews' "higher calling" had led to a snobbery and self-righteousness that came out in such inappropriate ways as the cursing psalms. These arguments did not endear Lewis to the Jewish community; not long ago *The Christian Century* published an article by a rabbi taking umbrage at Lewis's remarks.

Certainly Jesus introduced a new spirit ("You have heard it said . . . but I say unto you . . ."). But as Lewis himself notes, the Bible does not present such a clear-cut progression from the Old Testament to the New. Commands to love your enemies appear in the Old Testament as well. To complicate matters even further, New Testament authors quote approvingly some of the most problematic of the cursing psalms. For example, Peter applied one of the curses of Psalm 69 directly to Judas (Acts 1:20); Paul applied another ("May their eyes be darkened so they cannot see, and their backs be bent forever") to unbelieving Israel. Cursing psalms are not so easily dismissed.

In fact, the British scholar Deryck Sheriffs points out that C. S. Lewis himself changed as he underwent a personal trial late in life. Read *The Problem of Pain* and *A Grief Observed* back to back, and the change is obvious. The first book deals with suffering in the abstract and gives much philosophical insight into the role that pain plays in life. The second book, written after his wife died an excruciating death of bone cancer, reads in part like an extended imprecatory psalm. Lewis toyed with the notion of God as Cosmic Sadist, a torturer who slams a door in the faces of those who need him most. Lewis reflects in that journal,

> All that stuff about the Cosmic Sadist was not so much the expression of thought as of hatred. I was getting from it the only pleasure a man in anguish can get; the pleasure of hitting back. It was really just Billingsgate—mere abuse; "telling God what I thought of him."

I wonder what Lewis would have written about the cursing psalms after going through that personal ordeal.

3. The cursing psalms are best understood as prayers.

The cursing psalms appear in a considerably different light when we remember their literary context: We readers are "overhearing" prayers addressed to God. Seen in this way, the cursing psalms demonstrate what I have called "spiritual therapy" taken to its limits. As Dorothy Sayers once remarked, we all have diabolical thoughts, but there's a world of difference in responding with *words* instead of *deeds,* whether, say, we write a murder mystery or commit murder.

If a person wrongs me unjustly, I have several options. I can seek personal revenge, a response condemned by the Bible. I can deny or suppress my feelings of hurt and anger. Or I can take those feelings to God, entrusting God with the task of "retributive justice." The cursing psalms are vivid examples of that last option. "It is mine to avenge; I will repay," says the Lord—prayers like the cursing psalms place vengeance in the proper hands. Significantly, the cursing psalms express their outrage to God, not to the enemy.

Kathleen Norris, who struggled with the cursing psalms in her book *The Cloister Walk,* came to an accommodation with them in her later *Amazing Grace.* There she tells of inviting students in parochial schools to compose their own cursing psalms. Those who are picked on by their big brothers and sisters have a natural talent for imprecation, she found:

> One little boy wrote a poem called "The Monster Who Was Sorry." He began by admitting that he hates it when his father yells at him; his response in the poem is to throw his sister down the stairs, and then to wreck his room, and finally to wreck the whole town. The poem concludes: "Then I sit in my messy house and say to myself, 'I shouldn't have done all that.'"

If that boy had been a religious novice in the fourth-century monastic desert, adds Norris, his elders might have judged him well on the way toward repentance. Already he had become aware of the renovations necessary in the "messy house" before it became a place where God might dwell.

Instinctively, we want to "clean up" our feelings in our prayers, but perhaps we have it all backwards. Perhaps we should strive to take all our worst feelings to God. After all, what would be gossip when addressed to anyone else is petition when addressed to God. What is a vengeful curse when spoken about someone ("Damn those people!") is a plea of helpless dependence when spoken directly to God ("It's up to you to damn those people, since you only are a just judge").

I have made it a weekly practice, on a long walk on the hill behind my home, to present to God my anger against people who have wronged me. I recount all my reasons for feeling unfairly treated or misunderstood, forcing myself to open up deep feelings to God (does God not know them anyway?). I can testify that the outpouring itself has a therapeutic effect. Usually I come away feeling as if I have just released a huge burden. The unfairness no longer sticks like a thorn inside me, as it once did; I have expressed it aloud to someone—to God. Sometimes I find that in the process of expression, I grow in compassion. God's Spirit speaks to me of my own selfishness, my judgmental spirit, my own flaws that others have treated with grace and forgiveness, my pitifully limited viewpoint.

Miroslav Volf—a native Croatian who taught theology there during the war in the former Yugoslavia and who learned to identify with the cursing psalms very personally—explains in *Exclusion and Embrace* how those psalms may in fact lead toward forgiveness:

> For the followers of the crucified Messiah, the main message of the imprecatory Psalms is this: rage belongs before God. . . . This is no mere cathartic discharge of pent up aggression before the Almighty who ought to care. Much more significantly, by placing unattended rage before God we place both our unjust enemy and our own vengeful self face to face with a God who loves and does justice. Hidden in the dark chambers of our hearts and nourished by the system of darkness, hate grows and seeks to infest everything with its hellish will to exclusion. In the light of the justice and love of God, however, hate recedes and the seed is planted for the miracle of forgiveness.

Gradually, my weekly practice has expanded from a focus on myself to a sensitivity to others around me. Some weeks, I have no surface feelings of vengeance or resentment. Can I, though, use these psalms as insights into others who are suffering? What of countries that just got hit by hurricanes, floods, or droughts? Might Christians there be praying the psalms of desolation? What of my friends battling cancer? A woman living with an abusive husband? An alcoholic who cannot quite triumph? Can the difficult psalms help me enter into their struggles and perhaps pray the prayer on their behalf?

One reason I lean toward this way of understanding the cursing psalms is that I have read the end of the story in the book of Revelation. In that book we see a preview of a time when the most extreme of the cursing psalms will come true. Even the most notorious, Psalm 137, finds fulfillment: "With such violence the great city of Babylon will be thrown down, never to be found again" (Revelation 18:21). Justice will reign absolutely someday, and accomplishing that will require a time of cataclysmic violence against evil.

I see the cursing psalms as an important model for how to deal with evil and injustice. I should not try to suppress my reaction of horror and outrage at evil. Nor should I try to take justice in my own hands. Rather, I should deliver those feelings, stripped bare, to God. As the books of Job, Jeremiah, and Habakkuk clearly show, God has a high threshold of tolerance for what is appropriate to say in a prayer. God can "handle" my unsuppressed rage. I may well find that my vindictive feelings need God's correction—but only by taking those feelings to God will I have that opportunity for correction and healing.

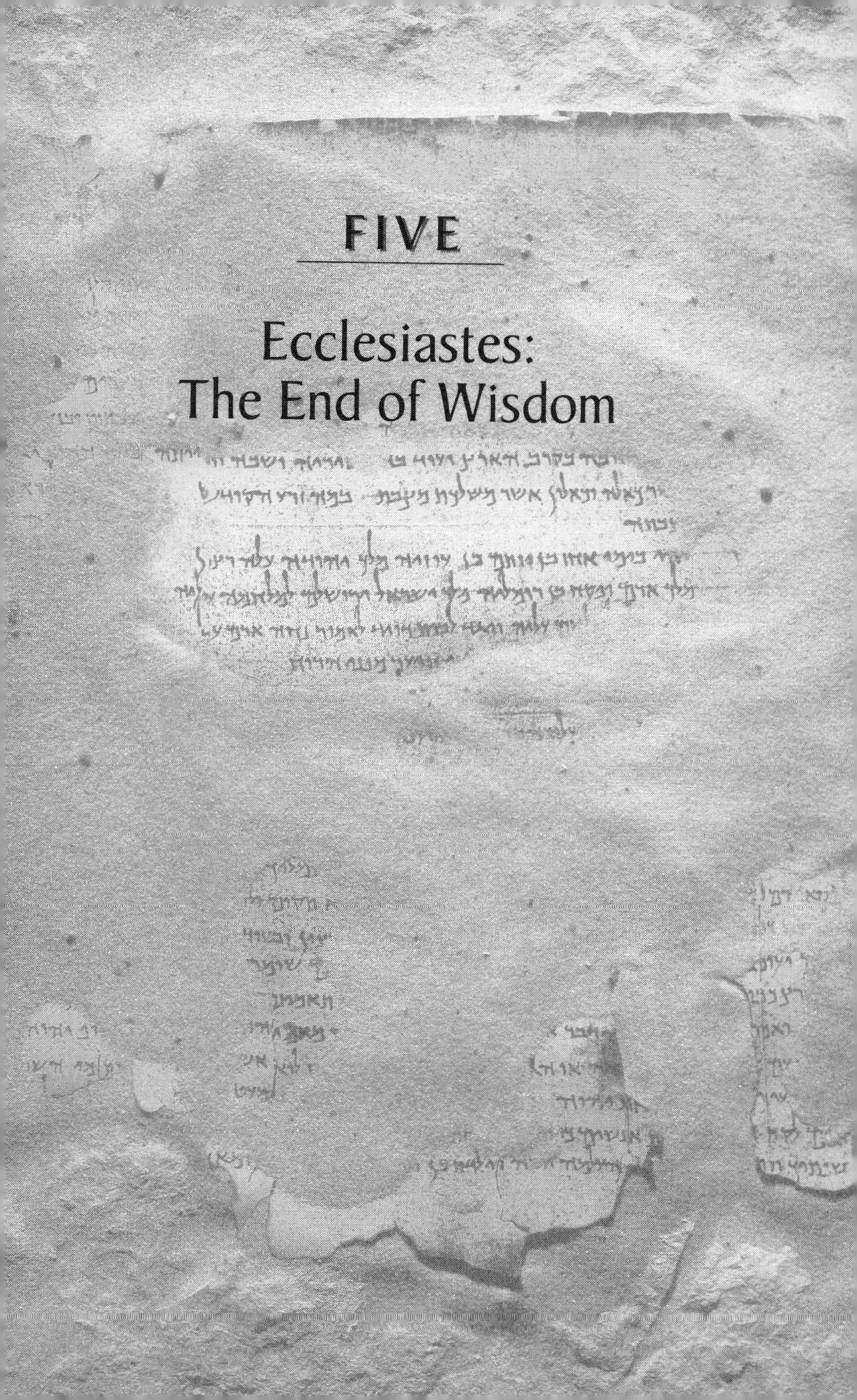

FIVE

Ecclesiastes: The End of Wisdom

FIVE

Ecclesiastes: The End of Wisdom

Ecclesiastes is, in some sense, a classical expression of utter bore-dom, though the boredom is set to such high counterpoint that its very expression is exciting. No one who can enjoy Ecclesiastes can be as bored as Ecclesiastes.

—CHARLES WILLIAMS

I first saw the word on the bright red cover of a book my elder brother brought home from college: *Existentialism Today.* Although I had no clue what *existentialism* meant, that book beckoned me into an arcane world of avant-garde philosophy. I had grown up in airtight fundamentalism, protected from exposure to such dangerous pollutants; the culture of Paris's Left Bank was as alien to me as that of Ouagadougou. Nevertheless, when as a teenager in the 1960s I read that red-covered book and went on to sample the novels of Camus and Sartre, something inside me stirred to life.

Flat emotions, a radical indifference to others, the sensation of drifting, numbness to pain, a resigned acceptance of a world gone mad—all these qualities had somehow seeped through the hermetic shield of fundamentalism. *That's me!* I thought as I read each book of existentialism. I was a child of my age after all.

Looking back now, I can see that I mainly identified with the despair. Why am I living? What is this circus all about? Can one person among five billion make a difference on this planet? Those questions pounded me like ocean waves as I read the writings of the French novelists, then Hemingway and Turgenev. All the turbulent questions of the Sixties washed over me, and existentialism provided an answer of sorts by insisting they have no answer. As I kept reading, I found that more current literature—John Updike, Kurt Vonnegut Jr., John Irving, Jerzy Kosinski, Walker Percy—gave off the same scent of futility, a scent stale as old cigar smoke.

"It makes little difference whether one dies at the age of thirty or threescore and ten," said Meursault in Camus's *The Stranger*, "since in either case, other men and women will continue living, the world will go on as before." What difference does anything make, really? It matters little whether you get up or stay in bed, whether you love life or hate it. Stab yourself in the hand, like Sartre's Mathieu, shoot a person in the hot Algerian sun like Camus's "Stranger," or just wander, Hemingwayesque, from one bar to another, picking fights. Life goes on whether you strive to change it or merely succumb to it. What is a human being, but a tiny blip in the billion-year progression of history?

Such is the predicament of modern literature, a predicament I wallowed in for a time. Carl Jung reported that a third of his cases suffered from no definable neurosis other than "the senselessness and emptiness of their lives." He went on to name meaninglessness the general neurosis of the modern era, as people torture themselves with questions that neither philosophy nor religion can answer.

Even now, decades later, I can slip back into an existentialist mode. When I travel overseas, for example, some link to reality disconnects, and I seem to float above humanity, observing from a lonely plateau how people in Japan or Egypt or wherever, in some ways like me and in some ways not, predictably sequence their lives. Children learn to communicate by talking about pooping and tinkling, then grow into repressed adults, then make their own children out of nothing but their own bodies, then in senile old age revert once again to conversation about pooping and tinkling. What is the point of this merry-go-round? How do we differ from other animals? Smarter than ants, surely, but far less cooperative. Why are we here?

G. K. Chesterton once wrote, "All men matter. You matter. I matter. It's the hardest thing in theology to believe."

The First Existentialist

A few years after my adolescent brush with existentialism, and after God had begun to heal some of my feelings of futility and despair, I discovered with an eerie shock precisely the same sentiments, of all places, in the center of the Bible. The mysterious, often-ignored book of Ecclesiastes contains every idea and emotion I had encountered in the writers of existential despair. Its author, the anonymous Teacher, looms as a larger-than-life figure, the wisest, richest, most powerful person of his day. The very first sentence of the book announces his conclusion about life:

> "Meaningless! Meaningless!"
> says the Teacher.
> "Utterly meaningless!
> Everything is meaningless."

That key word *meaningless* appears thirty-five times, drumming home the theme from beginning to end. (Elsewhere in the Bible the word occurs, not surprisingly, only in Job). It conveys a strong sense of "the absurd." The issues bothering the Teacher were the same ones that bothered Job, and that bother all fair-minded people today. The rich get richer and the poor poorer, evil people prosper as good ones suffer, tyrants reign, disasters happen, disease spreads, everyone dies and turns to dust. Life is unfair. Nothing makes sense; the whole world seems off-balance and twisted.

Forget prudence, concludes the Teacher. Eat, drink, and seize any fleeting moment of happiness. What else is the point of living? You work hard, and someone else gets all the credit. You struggle to be good, and bad people trample you. You accumulate money, and it goes to spoiled heirs. You seek pleasure, and it turns sour. Besides, everyone—rich or poor, good or evil—meets the same end: we all die. Death, the ever-present stalking specter, contradicts any notion that we are born to be happy. There is only one word fit to describe this life: meaningless!

To come across such words in Albert Camus is one thing, but in the Bible?

I wonder if the modern existentialists appreciate the delicious irony of Ecclesiastes 1:9–10, which declares, "There is nothing new under the sun," nothing "of which one can say, 'Look! This is something new.'" What seemed like brash iconoclasm in the 1960s, I learned, merely fulfilled the weary prophecies of the ancient Teacher who, three thousand years before, anticipated the full range of human experience and, astonishingly, included his findings in a book that became part of the Bible. As if to underscore the irony, about that time a musical group, the Byrds, released a best-selling single taken directly from Ecclesiastes 3: "There is a time for everything...." Truly, Ecclesiastes was a book for the ages and I began a search to understand this prescient volume.

Once I got over my sheer amazement about the message of Ecclesiastes, certain nagging questions set in. One struck me immediately, as I read the Old Testament straight through. How can Ecclesiastes coexist with its nearest neighbor, the book of

Proverbs? Two more unlike books could not be imagined. Read them back to back and you wonder whether Ecclesiastes was written as a kind of mocking rebuttal.

Proverbs has life figured out: Learn wisdom, exercise prudence, follow the rules, and you will live a long and prosperous life. Its tone of worldly optimism reminds me of Benjamin Franklin's aphorisms, and in fact today various industries produce early-American-style wall hangings featuring embroidered verses from Proverbs. Such industries, however, studiously avoid Ecclesiastes, for it depicts a world where none of the proverbs work out. The confident, matter-of-fact tone—*I've got life figured out and you need only follow this sage advice*—has vanished, replaced by resignation and cynicism. Thrifty, honorable people suffer and die just like everyone else. Evil people prosper and grow fat, regardless of Proverbs' neat formulas to the contrary.

> There is something else meaningless that occurs on earth: righteous men who get what the wicked deserve, and wicked men who get what the righteous deserve. This too, I say, is meaningless. (8:14)

For a glimpse of the stark disparity between Proverbs and Ecclesiastes, simply compare their use of the word *wisdom*. Proverbs exalts and personifies Wisdom, some would say with intentionally Messianic overtones. The Teacher's view of wisdom?

> For with much wisdom comes much sorrow;
> the more knowledge, the more grief. (1:18)

Wisdom has some advantages over folly, the Teacher grants, but so what? The same fate overtakes them both (2:13–14). "For who knows what is good for a man in life, during the few and meaningless days he passes through like a shadow? Who can tell him what will happen under the sun after he is gone?" (6:12).

This kind of disparity between two adjacent Old Testament books used to annoy and frustrate me. Shouldn't the Bible show more consistency? Over time, though, I came to appreciate the variety as one of the Old Testament's main strengths. Like a very long symphony, it ranges through joyful and somber moods, each contributing to the impact of the whole. It reflects what we all experience, sometimes the trials of Job and sometimes the serenity of Psalm 23, while living in a world that sometimes unfolds according to Proverbial principles and sometimes yields the jarring contradictions of Ecclesiastes.

The Curse of Getting What You Want

I also puzzled over the traditional identification of the Teacher with Solomon, the author of many of those proverbs. Most biblical scholars doubt that Solomon actually wrote Ecclesiastes (the book itself names no author, and various clues hint at a later date). Still, the book was clearly written under Solomon's shadow (see 1:1, 12, 16; 2:4–9; 7:26–29; 12:9). If a playwright today based a play on a president plagued by scandal who resigned from office under threat of impeachment, the play need not name Richard Nixon for the audience to get the point. Similarly, the whole tone of Ecclesiastes reflects the tenor of King Solomon's time, when Israel reached its zenith as a nation.

And there's the rub. How can the bleak despair of Ecclesiastes issue from the era of Israel's Golden Age, when things were going so well? The days of slavery in Egypt might produce such a gloomy volume, I reasoned, but not the glory days of Solomon and his royal successors. My reading of modern literature, in which I often heard overtones of Ecclesiastes, changed my assumptions.

It had always seemed odd to me that the modern existentialist philosophy of despair originated in one of the loveliest cities on earth, Paris, during a time of expanding wealth and opportunity. Curiously, I learned, existential despair, whether in the Teacher or in Camus, tends to sprout from the soil of excess. Why?

Walker Percy's book of essays, *The Message in the Bottle*, begins with examples of this anomaly. Percy asks a stream of questions, including these:

> Why do more people commit suicide in San Francisco, the most beautiful city in America, than in any other city? [In Europe, the suicide capital is Salzburg, Austria.]
>
> Why was it that Jean-Paul Sartre, sitting in a French café writing *Nausea*, which is about the absurdity of human existence and the nausea of life in the twentieth century—why was he the happiest man in France at the time?
>
> Why is it that a man riding a good commuter train from Larchmont to New York, whose needs and drives are satisfied, who has a good home, loving wife and family, good job, who enjoys unprecedented "cultural and recreational facilities," often feels bad without knowing why?

Percy goes on to explain that despair arises out of circumstances of plenty rather than deprivation. Indeed, I did not find alienation and despair in the grim, three-volume *Gulag Archipelago* by Solzhenitsyn; I found rage, a passion for justice, and a defiant will to survive. As Viktor Frankl explains in *Man's Search for Meaning*, the victims of the concentration camps, he among them, did not dare succumb to meaninglessness, for only an enduring faith in meaning kept them alive.

Existential despair did not germinate in the hell holes of Auschwitz or Siberia but rather in the cafes of Paris, the coffee shops of Copenhagen, the luxury palaces of Beverly Hills. After a trip into Eastern Europe during the Cold War, novelist Philip Roth reported, "In the West everything goes and nothing matters. While in the East, nothing goes and everything matters."

Paradoxically, then, a despairing book like Ecclesiastes will more likely emerge from a Golden Age. Consider the contrast between Ecclesiastes and Job. They cover many of the same themes—life's unfairness, why suffering exists, why evil people prosper and good ones suffer—but what a difference in tone! Ecclesiastes exudes meaninglessness and futility while Job rings with betrayal, passion, and a cry for justice. Job shakes his fist at God, calls him into account, demands a reply. The Teacher shrugs his shoulders, mumbles, "So what?" and reaches for another goblet of wine. The two define the spectrum of despair, from the anguish of unrelieved suffering to the decadent boredom of surfeit.

The tone of Ecclesiastes captures precisely the mood of affluent Western countries. Wendell Berry recalls the society of his comfortable U.S. upbringing as one in which

> we knew and took for granted: marriage without love; sex without joy; drink without conviviality; birth, celebration, and death without adequate ceremony; faith without doubt or trial; belief without deeds; manners without generosity. . . . Such humanizing emotions as pleasure in small profitless things, joy, wonder, ecstasy were removed as by an operation on the brain.

Or consider the scene in secular Europe where people drive BMWs and Volvos, eat in gourmet restaurants, visit sex shops, and pursue the good life. Having abandoned colonial ambitions, they even respond with tempered compassion to the latest international crisis of flood or famine. One would not call them wicked, yet they demonstrate no interest in God and no passion for morality. Such people outraged Job:

> They spend their years in prosperity
>   and go down to the grave in peace.
> Yet they say to God, "Leave us alone!
>   We have no desire to know your ways.

Who is the Almighty, that we should serve him?
What would we gain by praying to him?"

Ecclesiastes, though, toys with such a philosophy as an appealing model. According to Jack Miles, "Ecclesiastes neither curses nor blesses God but only finds him incomprehensible and does his best to hedge all bets, including any bet on wisdom or righteousness."

A clue into the origin of existential despair appears in a phrase early on in Ecclesiastes, when the Teacher exclaims, "What a heavy burden God has laid on men!" (1:13). He goes on to describe the burden in biographical detail. The Teacher's burden, unlike Job's, did not involve personal misfortune but was, to the contrary, a burden of excess. He attained great wisdom. He attempted social programs on a massive scale. He accumulated more wealth than anyone before him. He sought after every kind of pleasure. Yet in all these, he concluded at the end, "everything was meaningless, a chasing after the wind; nothing was gained under the sun" (2:11). All he got for his efforts was a fear of death and a bad case of insomnia. Why bother?

The Teacher never really expected to solve life's riddles, and his attitude of resignation contrasts sharply with Job's combativeness. Unlike Job, unlike so many of the psalmists, the Teacher apparently does not have a passionate relationship with God. He has slipped into idolatry: not the kind involving pagan statues, but the kind widespread in modern times, as in Western Europe where only a tiny fraction attend church of any type and people devote themselves instead to pursuing the "quality of life." Or the idolatry of the U.S., where, we insist, we have a guaranteed right to satisfy our pleasures, and nobody's going to stop us. The Teacher would agree, with this caveat: You'll never succeed, you'll always want more. Here is his conclusion:

> In this meaningless life of mine I have seen both of these:
>   a righteous man perishing in his righteousness,
>   and a wicked man living long in his wickedness.
>   Do not be overrighteous,
>   neither be overwise—
>   why destroy yourself?
>   Do not be overwicked,
>   and do not be a fool—
>   why die before your time?
>   It is good to grasp the one
>   and not let go of the other.

The Teacher's advice—be good but not too good, wise but not too wise—is a fine example of the search for a Golden Mean of behavior. After tasting the extremes on both sides, the Teacher settles in halfway between hedonism and suicide.

KGB Mole Theory

"What is the meaning of life?" asked the student of the rabbi.

The rabbi replied, "That's such a wonderful question, why would you want to exchange it for an answer?"

Apparent contradictions between Ecclesiastes and virtually everything else in the Bible eventually brought me back to the nagging question of how Ecclesiastes ever made it into the Bible. To understand the problem of Ecclesiastes, consider the following verses, removed from their contexts but each expressing a point of view espoused by the Teacher:

> Consider what God has done:
>   Who can straighten
>   what he has made crooked? (7:13)

> Go, eat your food with gladness, and drink your wine with a joyful heart, for it is now that God favors what you do. (9:7)

A feast is made for laughter,
and wine makes life merry,
but money is the answer for everything. (10:19)

Whatever your hand finds to do, do it with all your might,
for in the grave, where you are going, there is neither
working nor planning nor knowledge nor wisdom. (9:10)

Each of these statements represents a stage in the Teacher's
pilgrimage-in-reverse as he investigates the meaning of life, and
each radically contradicts other parts of the Bible. Why would
the Teacher devote pages of detail to express each vain philosophy while including a mere sprinkling of sentences to present the more common biblical point of view?

Conservative commentaries I have consulted use some vari-
ation of what I call the "KGB mole" approach to Ecclesiastes. In
the last months of the Cold War, an important KGB official
defected to the U.S. He appeared on the evening news extolling
the virtues of American democracy and was given spacious
grounds in Virginia on which to live happily ever after. A few
months later, however, he bolted to the Soviet embassy,
renounced his defection, and declared all his words of praise to
have been lies.

Many commentaries present Ecclesiastes as a comparable
set-up job. The author, a genuine believer, who certainly cannot be in the throes of despair himself, is taking on the guise
of a secular person, one "under the sun" (a phrase used thirty
times). He does so merely to lead the reader along, meanwhile
demonstrating the futility of life under the sun. Then at the end
he springs the trap and—*Gotcha!*—announces the truth he has
believed all along: "Fear God and keep his commandments, for
this is the whole duty of man" (12:13).

The apologist Francis Schaeffer perfected a similar
approach, which he termed "taking people to the logical extent
of their presuppositions." For the sake of argument he would

adopt the most materialistic assumptions—there is no God, there are no absolutes—and then show that such thinking leads to the logical extremes of suicide and anarchy. Many people found Schaeffer's approach convincing. Some might argue that the Russian novelists Turgenev and Dostoevsky used a similar approach in *Fathers and Sons, The Brothers Karamazov,* and *The Possessed.* Both authors stretch the presuppositions of nihilism (a word coined by Turgenev) to their logical extent, exposing philosophy's weakness as a moral rule for societies or individuals. "If there is no God, everything is permitted," wrote Dostoevsky.

This legitimate method of apologetics, however, proves unsatisfying when applied to Ecclesiastes for one basic reason: in Ecclesiastes, the "secular" or meaningless portions are far more convincing than the few rays of light. Just as Milton unwittingly made Satan the true hero of *Paradise Lost,* the Teacher makes the despairing portions of Ecclesiastes the most compelling parts of the book. The more optimistic or "devotional" portions seem stitched-in, the Teacher's thinly disguised attempts to talk himself into hope. To appreciate the book's worth, I had to search deeper, mining the Teacher's strange philosophy from the inside.

Burden of the Gods

The only wisdom we can hope to acquire is the wisdom of humility. Humility is endless.

—T. S. ELIOT

Chapter 3 of Ecclesiastes provides, in my view, the heart of the Teacher's message. It begins with the most famous passage in the book, the poem celebrated in the folk song from the sixties ("There is a time for everything . . ."), and then repeats the phrase already cited: "I have seen the burden God has laid on men." Next comes a remarkable section that sets a course for all that follows.

The Teacher develops what theologians used to call, before concern about sexist language, "Anthropology: the doctrine of man." He considers in what ways human beings resemble animals—we all meet the same fate—and in what ways we differ. Primarily, he says, we differ by bearing the burden of the gods. As Pascal put it, the greatness of man compared to animals is that he knows himself to be miserable.

The Greeks expressed this "burden" in their myth of Prometheus, who brought humanity fire, symbolizing enlightenment and the arts. By doing so he also brought them "honors beyond their due," and for punishment Zeus chained Prometheus to a rock, to be eviscerated by an eagle. Humans thus overreached, bringing on themselves the weight of suffering and guilt.

In a striking parallel to the Greek myth, Christians likewise believe that God laid that burden on us because we grasped for it. Recall the Garden of Eden, before even a whiff of existential despair, when work and pleasure were wholly satisfying. In that time of human bliss Adam and Eve sought "to be like God, understanding good and evil." They chose to deny their creatureliness by reaching for more than God had granted them. Distrusting God, they brought the burden of the gods upon themselves.

Our own century has poignantly partaken of the burden of the gods, discovering both its exalted hopes and its crushing despair. Most of our problems have come about, ironically, because of our desire to progress, to improve, to make life better. At the end of the nineteenth century, it looked as if science and technology would cure disease, banish pain, and allow us all to live like kings. But the progress that brought us dishwashers and Salk vaccines also brought us nuclear weapons, global warming, and carcinogens without number.

The late Bruno Bettelheim remarked:

Never before have so many had it so good; no longer do we tremble in fear of sickness or hunger, of hidden evils in the dark, of the spell of witches. The burden of killing toil has been lifted from us, and machines, not the labor of our hands, will soon provide us with nearly all we need, and much that we don't really need. We have inherited freedoms man has striven after for centuries. Because of all this and much more we should be living in a dawn of great promise. But now that we are freer to enjoy life, we are deeply frustrated in our disappointment that the freedom and comfort, sought with such deep desire, do not give meaning and purpose to our lives.

Our best attempts backfire. We learn to prolong life, yet fail to provide meaning for the people permanently attached to the whirring machines—and so Kevorkians arise with alternative solutions. We bring antibiotics to underdeveloped countries, only to see the infant mortality rates plummet, populations soar, and the specter of famine rear up. We dump a hundred billion dollars into a War on Poverty and end up with more poor people than ever before.

The most technologically advanced countries are also the ones marked by family breakdown, drug addiction, abortion, violent crime, homelessness, and suicide. As Malcolm Muggeridge lamented,

The result is almost invariably the exact opposite of what's intended. Thus, expanding public education has served to increase illiteracy; half a century of pacifist agitation has resulted in the two most ferocious and destructive wars of history, political egalitarianism has made for a heightened class-consciousness . . . and sexual freedom has led to erotomania on a scale hitherto undreamed of.

—*Jesus Rediscovered*

Similarly, Ecclesiastes sounded its note of doom in an era of unprecedented prosperity and social progress. The ruler over Israel could sense within himself and his nation the failure to sustain the burden. He learned the hard lesson Moses had tried to teach the Israelites centuries before: whatever humans touch will bear a fatal flaw. Good times represent the real danger; our best efforts spell ruin. In short, human beings are not gods, and that realization drove the Teacher to despair. Roger Shattuck calls it "the wife of Bath effect," after Chaucer's character: "We are discontent with our lot, whatever it is, just because it is ours."

Eternity in Our Hearts

I once came across a scene of beauty just a few miles outside Anchorage, Alaska, where I noticed a number of cars pulled off the highway. Against the slate-gray sky, the water of an ocean inlet had a slight greenish cast, interrupted by small whitecaps. Soon I saw these were not whitecaps at all, but whales—silvery white beluga whales in a pod feeding no more than fifty feet offshore. I stood with the other onlookers for forty minutes, listening to the rhythmic motion of the sea, following the graceful, ghostly crescents of surfacing whales. The crowd was hushed, even reverent. For just that moment, nothing else— dinner reservations, the trip schedule, life back home—mattered. We were confronted with a scene of quiet beauty and a majesty of scale. We felt small. We strangers stood together in silence until the whales moved farther out. Then we climbed the bank together and got in our cars to resume our busy, ordered lives that suddenly seemed less urgent.

The Teacher would doubtless understand the crowd's response to the whales, for he insists that though we are not gods, we are not solely animals either. God "has also set eternity in the hearts of men." Such an elegant phrase applies to much in human experience. Surely it hints at a religious instinct, an instinct that, to the bafflement of anthropologists, finds expression in every human society ever studied. Our hearts perceive eternity in ways other than religious as well. The Teacher is no nihilist; he sees with dazzling clarity the beauty in the created world.

I detect in Ecclesiastes a sense of the "longing," or *Sehnsucht,* that C. S. Lewis wrote about so eloquently. "Drippings of grace," Lewis called them once, those rumors of transcendence that he experienced when listening to music, reading Greek myths, or visiting a cathedral. We all feel that longing sometimes: in sex, in beauty, in music, in nature, in love.

Where did our sense of beauty and pleasure come from? That seems to me a huge question—the philosophical equivalent, for atheists, to the problem of pain for Christians. The Teacher's answer is clear: A good and loving God naturally would want his creatures to experience delight, joy, and personal fulfillment. G. K. Chesterton credits pleasure, or eternity in his heart, as the signpost that eventually directed him to God:

> There had come into my mind a vague and vast impression that in some way all good was a remnant to be stored and held sacred out of some primordial ruin. Man had saved his good as [Robinson] Crusoe saved his goods: he had saved them from a wreck. All this I felt and the age gave me no encouragement to feel it. And all this time I had not even thought of Christian theology.
>
> —*Orthodoxy*

An encounter with beauty or an experience of intense joy may cause us for a time to forget our true mortal state—but not for long. The child we held in our lap at dinnertime we scream at near bedtime; the person we made love to last night we feud with today. Every bride walks the aisle believing in a new life of bliss, and every parent of a newborn leaves the hospital full of joy; yet we know that half of all marriages end in divorce and perhaps a third of all children will suffer abuse at their parents' hands. We cannot shed, ever, the unbearable burden of the gods.

A person may, of course, sense eternity in the heart and never turn to the God who placed it there. For those who continue to live "under the sun" the Teacher of Ecclesiastes has a simple message: you will surely fail to find what satisfies. "Is that all there is?" asked singer Peggy Lee in her own Sixties' version of Ecclesiastes. You may fail on the positive side by frantically chasing wealth, success, and gourmet sex, or you may fail on the negative side by dropping out, giving up, and sinking into a chemical stupor. In his odyssey, the Teacher fell both ways.

The account of decadence by the richest, wisest, most talented person in the world serves as a perfect allegory for what can happen when we lose sight of the Giver whose good gifts we enjoy. Pleasure represents a great good but also a grave danger. If we start chasing pleasure as an end in itself, along the way we may lose sight of the One who gave us such good gifts as sexual drive, taste buds, and the capacity to appreciate beauty. In that event, as Ecclesiastes tells it, a wholesale devotion to pleasure will paradoxically lead to a state of utter despair.

Ecclesiastes insists that the stones we trip over are good things in themselves: "He has made everything beautiful in its time" (3:11). Yet, by assuming a burden we were not meant to carry, we turn nudity into pornography, wine into alcoholism, food into gluttony, and human diversity into racism and prejudice. Despair descends as we abuse God's good gifts; they seem no longer gifts, and no longer good.

Ecclesiastes endures as a work of great literature and a book of great truth because it presents both sides of life on this planet: the promise of pleasures so alluring that we may devote our lives to their pursuit, and then the haunting realization that these pleasures ultimately do not satisfy. God's tantalizing world is too big for us. Made for another home, made for eternity, we finally realize that nothing this side of timeless Paradise will quiet the rumors of discontent.

The Teacher completes his sentence: "He has also set eternity in the hearts of men; yet they cannot fathom what God has done from beginning to end." That is the point of Ecclesiastes in a nutshell. The same lesson Job learned in dust and ashes— that we humans cannot figure out life on our own—the Teacher learns in a robe and palace. In the end, the Teacher freely admits that life does not make sense outside of God and will never fully make sense because we are not God. As Kierkegaard remarked, "If a man's life is not to be dozed away in inactivity or wasted in bustling movement, there must be something higher which draws it."

In the Teacher's words,

As you do not know the path of the wind,
    or how the body is formed in a mother's womb,
so you cannot understand the work of God,
    the Maker of all things. (11:5)

Unless we acknowledge our limits and subject ourselves to God's rule, unless we trust the Giver of all good gifts, we will end up in a state of despair. Ecclesiastes calls us to accept our status as creatures under the dominion of the Creator, something few of us do without a struggle.

A Tale of Two Kingdoms

You know, it's a funny thing that when you're very old, as I am, seventy-five and near to dying, the queerest thing happens. You very often wake up about two or three in the morning and you are half in and half out of your body, a most peculiar situation. You can see your battered old carcass there between the sheets and it's quite a tossup whether you resume full occupancy and go through another day or make off where you can see, like the lights in the sky as you're driving along, the lights of Augustine's

City of God. *In that sort of limbo, between being in and out of your body, you have the most extraordinary confidence, a sharpened awareness that this earth of ours with all its inadequacies is an extraordinary, beautiful place, that the experience of living in it is a wonderful, unique experience, that relations with other human beings, human love, human procreation, work, all these things are marvelous and wonderful despite all that can be said about the difficulty of our circumstances; and finally, a conviction passing all belief that as a participant in his purposes for his creation and that those purposes are loving and not malign, and creative and not destructive, are universal and not particular. In that confidence is an incredible comfort and an incredible joy.*

—MALCOLM MUGGERIDGE, *THE END OF CHRISTENDOM*

Not many sermons get preached on Ecclesiastes, for it is one of the Bible's most confusing books. Many conservative Christians treat it with polite distaste, as if it had sneaked into the canon when no one was looking. I have come to see Ecclesiastes not as a mistake, nor as a contrived form of reverse apologetics, rather as a profound reminder of the limits of being human. Ecclesiastes sets forth the inevitable consequences of a life without God at the center, and the pitfalls it warns against endanger the believer as much as the pagan. King Solomon, the shadow figure behind the book, offers the best example of all.

From Genesis 12 onward, the Old Testament records how God fulfilled his covenant with Abraham. First God set aside a tribe, the Israelites, and then through a tortuous process made of them a great people. After the Exodus from Egypt, they gained their own land, the last of the promises to be fulfilled. In Solomon's day, the united nation had peace and prosperity. The climax came in an astounding close-encounter-of-the-third-kind scene recorded in 1 Kings 8, when the glory of the Lord swooped down to fill Solomon's temple. In Solomon's day, everything was working. Jews were bringing light to the Gentiles: a parade of

foreign rulers from Sheba and elsewhere came to see for themselves the wonders of Israel and Israel's God. Solomon's reign
stands out as a shining moment of tranquility in the tormented
history of the Jews.

No one in history started out with greater advantages than
King Solomon, with his privileges of birth, his enormous natural
talent, and a supernatural gift of wisdom. Yet not even Solomon
with all his wisdom could bear the burden of the gods. His sexual excesses were legendary: seven hundred wives and three
hundred concubines. First Kings describes the seven-year construction of God's temple in elaborate detail, then pointedly
notes that Solomon's palace, twice the temple's size, took twice
as long to build. It was Solomon who first placed pagan idols
in the sacred places of Jerusalem, in an attempt to placate his
exotic wives. The earnest ruler who had showed such promise
ended up defying all of God's rules against a king's excesses.
The author of three thousand proverbs broke them with an
immoderation that has never been equaled.

The nation split in two after Solomon's death and slid
toward ruin from that day on. As Moses had predicted long
before, Israel's finest hour led to its precipitous decline and fall.
Ecclesiastes, reflecting the beginning of that decline, comes to
us as the hardest lesson learned in the streets of Jerusalem. It
is, in short, a profound summary of the "city of man" versus the
"city of God," the kingdom of this world versus the kingdom of
heaven.

Is it possible that God permitted the entire tragic experiment of Israel's nationhood in order to prove a point about the
visible kingdom—about any visible kingdom? Solomon, with
every advantage of wisdom, power, and wealth—all good gifts
from God—led his nation to destruction. Did God grant
Solomon those advantages in order to put to death illusions and
thus prepare the way for a new kingdom? Kingdoms of this
world are built on intelligence, beauty, wealth, and strength.

Yet even at their best, their Solomonic best, such human attractions fail. Has not history born out that truth again and again, world without end?

A later king—one greater than Solomon, he claimed—established his rule instead among the lame and poor and oppressed and ritually unclean. He belittled Solomon's glory by comparing it to that of a common day lily. He offered no rewards other than the prospect of an executioner's cross. Solomon's kingdom succeeds by accumulation; Jesus' kingdom succeeds by self-sacrifice. "You must lose yourself to find yourself" was Jesus' most-repeated proverb. The world was still not ready for Jesus' kind of kingdom. Even when he returned to earth after resurrection the disciples did not grasp the difference: "Lord, are you at this time going to restore the kingdom to Israel?" they asked, still yearning for the visible kingdom of Solomon.

The kings of Israel who followed Solomon did not learn, the disciples who followed Jesus did not learn, and what of us? I can envision the Teacher of Ecclesiastes standing before the magazine rack of a modern newsstand. "All these body-building magazines—*Shape, New Body, Muscle and Fitness*—do you think flesh lasts forever? Have you no thought for the grave? *Success, Inc., Entrepreneur*—what are you scrambling for? Do you truly believe you will find satisfaction there? *Mad, Lampoon, Atlantic, Harper's*—I tried folly as well as wisdom, and both lead to the same place. To the grave." In Jesus' cryptic words, which could stand as a summary for the message of Ecclesiastes, "What good is it for a man to gain the whole world, yet forfeit his soul?"

Ecclesiastes has an eerily modern ring to it because we have not learned its most basic lessons. We too chase the allure of the visible kingdom.

Existentialist writers popular in the Sixties proved prophetic in one sense: they examined the illusions we live under and exposed them as illusions. In one sense the restless, those who sense the world's disharmony, are closer to God than those satisfied in the world. In Walker Percy's words, human alienation is "first and last the homelessness of a man who is not in fact at home." Unlike the Teacher, most modern writers blame God, or the lack of God, for the human condition. Few instead perceive despair as a symptom of our humble need for God. They do not show us the home for which we were created to belong.

The End of the Matter

The Jews have a custom of remembering Ecclesiastes once a year, during the Festival of Tents. When I lived in Chicago, families along the North Shore erected tents in the backyards of their suburban homes, inside which they ate meals and reflected on the Old Testament accounts of their ancestors in the Sinai wilderness. In the midst of that ceremony, a leader stood among them and read the entire book of Ecclesiastes aloud. It served as a sober warning against depending on their success and prosperity.

Perhaps we should all adopt the Jewish practice of an annual reading, especially we Americans in our condominiums and gated communities, surrounded by the bounty of the visible kingdom, smugly reassured by the triumph of capitalism, our nation secure behind its shield of nuclear weapons. J. I. Packer calls Ecclesiastes the "one book in Scripture that is expressly designed to turn us into realists."

For committed Christians as well, Ecclesiastes offers a corrective. At times we may find that faith has gone dead, that the answers we cling to no longer seem to offer a solution to life. We may feel depression, despair, boredom, apathy. Or, at the other extreme, we may feel tempted by a happy-face spirituality that promises health and prosperity, or by a spiritual asceticism that denies the value of food, drink, relaxation, and lovemaking. To counter all these tendencies, Ecclesiastes holds up the stark solution of dis-illusioned realism. We cradle eternity in our hearts but bear the burden of the gods on our shoulders.

Ecclesiastes is not the whole revelation, of course. It says nothing of the Covenant and includes no miracle stories of God's intervention or promises of God's ultimate deliverance. The Teacher maintains a narrow range of vision, confined to what he sees around him. Even so, the book of Ecclesiastes concludes with this warning:

> Now all has been heard;
>> here is the conclusion of the matter:
> Fear God and keep his commandments,
>> for this is the whole duty of man.
> For God will bring every deed into judgment,
>> including every hidden thing,
>> whether it is good or evil.

Some view the final chapter as a form of invitation hymn, as if the author had disingenuously led us along toward a final appeal. Some see it as a later addition, tacked on by scribes worried about the overall message of Ecclesiastes. I get a different image, of a tired old man, not unlike Solomon, who has earnestly sought the answer to the riddles of life. In the first part of chapter 12, he gives a brilliant, Shakespearean depiction of aging. Now, overwhelmed by his mistakes and his mortality, he sighs and says: Only one thing is worthwhile. Somehow, in the midst of this meaningless world, remember your Creator.

In the words of philosopher Ludwig Wittgenstein, "To believe in a God means to see that the facts of this world are not the end of the matter. To believe in God means to see that life has a meaning... That this meaning does not lie in it but outside it." David and the other psalmists made a habit of assembling every aspect of their lives to present to God as an act of worship. The Teacher did the opposite, atomizing such things as work and pleasure into their constituent parts so completely that

165

he found them nearly impossible to reassemble. He peeled the onion's layers until he found nothing left. Hence the warnings— Remember your Creator, Fear God—for those who still had time to heed them.

The existentialist writers popularized the phrase "leap of faith" as a way of describing the plunge beyond our cultural assumptions to a belief in transcendence. Those with religious sensibilities found a kinsman in Søren Kierkegaard, champion of Abraham, Job, David, and all such Knights of Faith who believed against all odds, despite doubts to the contrary. One of the existentialist writers sent me back to the seventeeth-century mathematician and philosopher Blaise Pascal, who also struggled with issues of meaninglessness. Pascal concluded that faith sometimes resembles a wager. He told his friends, "If I believe in God and life after death and you do not, and if there is no God, we both lose when we die. However, if there is a God, you still lose and I gain everything." I think the Teacher would have approved.

The cry at the end of Ecclesiastes is not a triumphalist "See, I told you so!" but rather the last gasp of an extraordinary person who spent his life in pursuit of every possible alternative. I detect in that cry the tone of François Mauriac's *Viper's Tangle* or of Graham Greene's *The Power and the Glory*—in short, the weary tone of despair that characterizes our century. If you are trapped in the visible world, and insist on seeing nothing else, cold logic will lead you toward meaninglessness and despair. Are we, as Mark Twain suggested, on a "plodding sad pilgrimage, this pathetic drift between the eternities"? Somehow, the Teacher counsels at the end, take the leap of faith and believe that there is a God, and that this life will make sense one day: when the eternity in our hearts will find its Sabbath rest, when the burden of the gods will settle on our resurrected shoulders with a bearable lightness of being.

I don't know Who—or What—put the question. I don't know when it was put. I don't even remember answering. But at some moment I did answer Yes *to Someone—or Something—and from that hour I was certain that existence is meaningful and that, therefore, my life, in self-surrender, had a goal.*

—DAG HAMMARSKJÖLD, *MARKINGS*

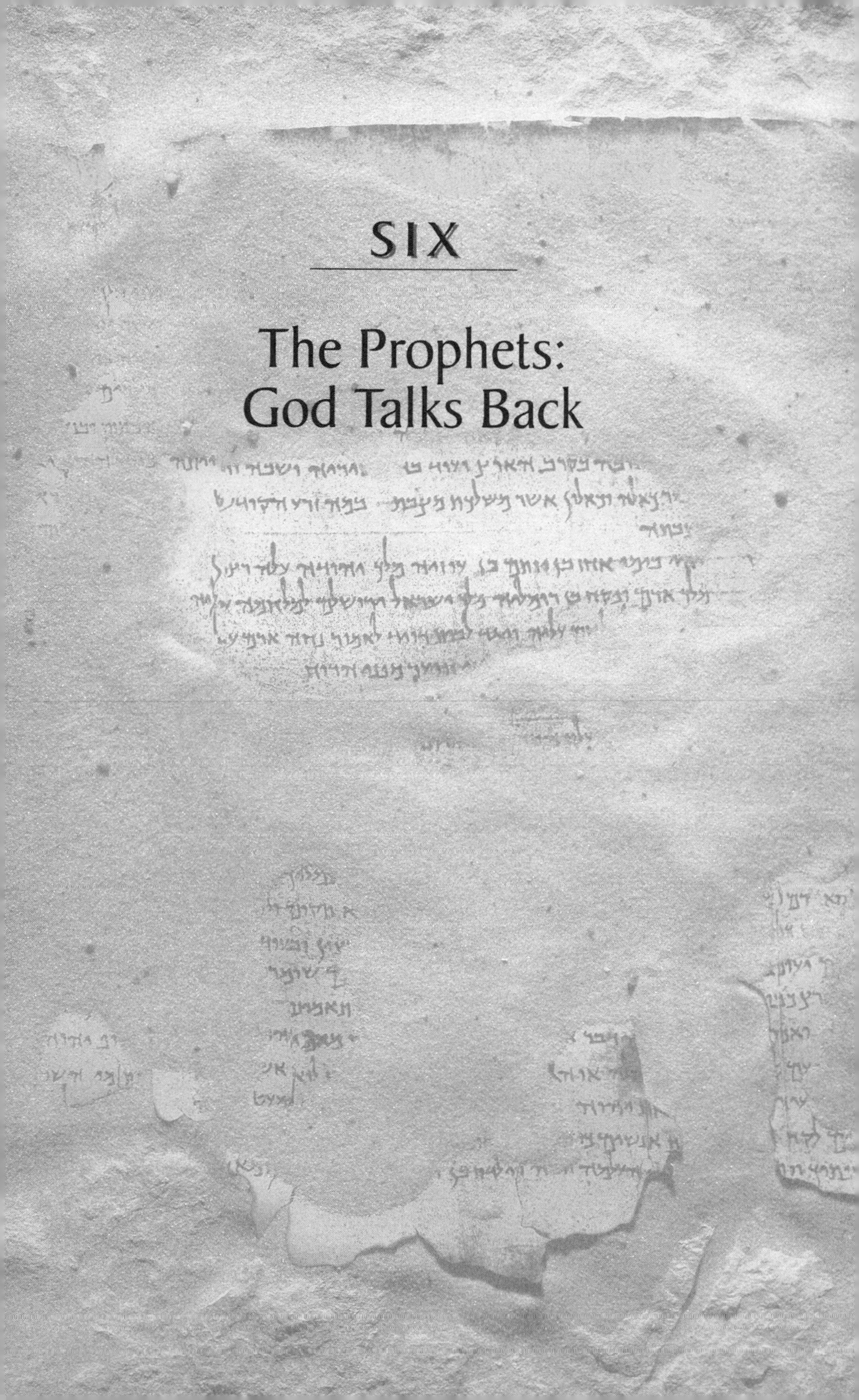

SIX

The Prophets: God Talks Back

SIX

The Prophets: God Talks Back

*The situation of a person immersed in the prophets' words is one
of being exposed to a ceaseless shattering of indifference, and one
needs a skull of stone to remain callous to such blows.*

—ABRAHAM HESCHEL

If you examine the Bibles of even the most diligent students
you may find a telltale band of white on the paper edges just
over halfway through, a mark of cleanness indicating how sel-
dom fingers touch the Old Testament prophets. Although those
seventeen books fill about a fifth of the Bible's bulk, they tend
to go unread. Why? I put that question to a Bible study class,
and a graduate student bluntly summed up the class's sentiments: "The prophets are weird and confusing, and they all
sound alike." As I thought about his answer, I realized he had
captured the very problems that kept me away from the
prophets for many years.

Weird, yes. I gained my first impressions as a child at summer "prophecy conferences." Large banners hung across the
platform: white bed sheets stitched together and covered with
crude drawings of science-fiction-looking creatures. The drawings mostly depicted visions from Daniel and Revelation, and
speakers wielding long pointers would expound on the meaning of the various toes and horns and eyes. They were a strange

lot, the prophets. As Jack Miles observes, "The three major prophets—Isaiah, Jeremiah, and Ezekiel—may be considered, respectively, the manic, the depressive, and the psychotic articulation of the prophetic message. As for calm, sane, moderate visions of prophecy, in effect, there are none."

Confusing? Indeed. Each prophecy conference speaker had a private theory on how many months we Christians would have to suffer during the Tribulation, and where on earth the Antichrist was growing up even as we met together. When the European Common Market began to form, excitement really heated up—the ten toes of Daniel's beast!—only to calm down a bit when the eleventh and twelfth members gained admittance.

Later, as I read church history, I learned that Christians had bet on the wrong horses in the 1940s when Hitler, Stalin, and Mussolini seemed to vie for the role of Antichrist; and in the 1840s when believers gathered on mountaintops to await Christ's return; and in the 1400s and the 400s and even in the first century A.D. Such luminaries as Jonathan Edwards, Martin Luther, and Isaac Newton made solemn declarations about the fulfillment of prophecy that now appear foolish.

I remember Salem Kirban identifying the invasion of African "killer bees" into the United States as a fulfillment of Revelation 9, presaging the sign of the fifth trumpet. I also remember in the 1980s hearing Hal Lindsey relate a spy scandal to biblical prophecy. Toshiba's leak of a milling system to the Leningrad shipyards, he claimed, had made Soviet subs undetectable by the U.S., thus moving the world much closer to the end times. I haven't heard from Lindsey recently (his book *The Late Great Planet Earth* was the best-selling book of the 1970s, bar none), except to note that much of his attention has turned from Russia to Iraq. A friend of mine cynically commented that the reason James Dobson grew so popular is that Hal Lindsey proved wrong about the end of the world: Christians suddenly realized they had enough time left to raise families.

Recently, a passel of new books has come out pegging key events to the year 2000, which echoes the hysteria from the year 1000. Prophecy "experts" are now warning about red heifers being secretly bred in Israel, about computer systems in Belgium programmed to keep track of "the mark of the beast," and about United Nations troops being smuggled into U.S. military bases.

All the prognosticators in history have given impressive reasons why the coded prophecies in the Bible would find fulfillment in their own day, and so far all have proved wrong. Should that surprise us? Jewish scribes had several centuries to pore over the prophecies of Jesus' birth and life, passages that seem crystal-clear to believers today, and not one of them came up with accurate predictions of the Messiah's First Coming. Why should we expect to do any better with the Second Coming? Thinking such thoughts, I confess, used to make me skeptical of reading the prophets at all: if no one can agree on their meaning, why read them?

"They all sound alike." This last complaint, I confess, posed the biggest obstacle to my reading the prophets. They seemed boring. Through the forms of preaching, poetry, politics, and literature, all of them gave variations of the same two-liner message: "It's going to get bad, real bad. Then it will get much better." In short, when I thought about the prophets at all, I had the image of fusty old men wagging their fingers at the world, the same image that has inspired countless caricatures in magazine cartoons.

Thoroughly Modern Books

For these reasons my Bible too showed a broad band of white after the poetry books, signifying unread portions, until one day my work on *The Student Bible* called for a close reading of them. My job now *required* me to study the prophets. A surprising thing happened over time: I experienced an abrupt turnabout, so abrupt that I may now claim the prophets as my favorite section of the entire Bible.

Far from my prior stereotype of fusty finger-waggers, I found the prophets to be the most "modern" writers imaginable. In chapter after chapter they deal with the very same themes that hang like a cloud over our century: the silence of God, economic disparity, injustice, war, the seeming sovereignty of evil, the unrelieved suffering that afflicts our world. These, the same themes that surface periodically in Job, Psalms, Ecclesiastes, and even Deuteronomy, the prophets bring into sharp focus, as if examining them under a microscope. Prototypal books of Old Testament realism, the prophets eloquently express the doubts, pains, and complexities that we all feel—that I feel. I came to see them as acute witnesses to the dilemma of being human.

Isaiah, normally a towering giant of faith, lamented at one point, "Truly you are a God who hides himself." Another time he cried out in near-despair, "Oh, that you would rend the heavens and come down!"

Most of Habakkuk comprises a loud complaint to God, beginning with words that resound in modern skeptics:

> How long, O Lord, must I call for help,
>   but you do not listen?
> Or cry out to you, "Violence!"
>   but you do not save?
> Why do you make me look at injustice?
>   Why do you tolerate wrong?

Malachi and Jeremiah loudly protested the failure of "success theology." In their day, God's prophets were no longer, like Elijah, blasting enemies with fire from the sky; they were moldering in dungeons and wells, if not being sawed in half. Jeremiah, who, after all, bequeathed us the English word *jeremiad,* filled the longest book in the Bible with a message squeezed out between sobs.

Oh that my head were a spring of water
    and my eyes a fountain of tears!
My heart is broken within me;
    all my bones tremble.
I am like a drunken man,
    like a man overcome by wine.

Oh, my anguish, my anguish!
    I writhe in pain.
Oh, the agony of my heart!
    My heart pounds within me,
    I cannot keep silent.

What caused such existential torment? Beyond his own pain and that of his people, Jeremiah agonized over the apparent powerlessness of God. He challenged God directly: "Why are you like a man taken by surprise, like a warrior powerless to save?" The agnostic philosopher Voltaire could not have phrased it better. How can an all-powerful and all-loving God tolerate such a messed-up world?

To the prophets, God seemed to be pulling farther and farther away from his creation. Why do godless nations flourish? they asked. Why so many natural disasters? Why such poverty and depravity in the world, and so few miracles? Where are you, God? Why don't you speak to us, as you used to. Show yourself, break your silence. For God's sake, literally, *act!*

God Speaks Up

The most amazing feature of the prophets, and the reason these seventeen books merit close study, is that God answers the prophets' bracing questions. He storms and explodes, defending the way he runs the world. He blocks their complaints with some complaints of his own.

Imagine a biographer stumbling across seventeen long letters from Abraham Lincoln addressed to his wife, his generals, and his secretary of state, revealing his innermost thoughts during the crisis times of the Civil War. Some of the letters would cover the same ground, of course, but using different words and tone depending on when he wrote them and to whom. Historians would dissect every fragment for insight into the inner workings of America's greatest president. Why did he make this decision and not that one, act here and not there? The prophets offer such a window into the mind of God.

In an ironic twist, God points to the prophets themselves—the very people who are questioning his hiddenness—as proof of his concern. "Surely he does nothing without revealing his plan to his servants the prophets." How can a nation complain about the silence of God when they have the likes of Ezekiel, Jeremiah, Daniel, Isaiah?

The prophets were calling for miraculous displays of God's power, as in the days of Moses. Yet the verdict was in: as Deuteronomy records, Israel had responded to those miraculous signs with stubborn rebellion. Why repeat the past? Now, through the prophets, God turns instead to the power of the word. Evidently God does not consider "mere words" an inferior form of proof, for he chose the prophets to communicate the anguish God himself felt. Poor Jeremiah longed for another mode of expression; God's word, he said, "is in my heart like a fire, a fire shut up in my bones. I am weary of holding it in; indeed I cannot."

I can barely begin to mention God's specific replies to the prophets' questions. He tells of the value of pruning an unruly plant (or nation), points with pride to a remnant of faithful followers, recounts historical proofs of his love, promises a Messiah-deliverer, and concludes always with a preview of the future when all that is wrong on earth will be set right. Beyond such rational explanations, one important message shines through with great force: God passionately desires his people.

Above all else, the prophets repeat the constant refrain of the Old Testament, that we *matter* to God.

On the one hand, the prophets describe the majestic power of a God who creates solar systems with a word and tosses empires like kindling sticks. On the other hand, they proclaim God's intimate, personal involvement with his chosen people and with individual human beings. Abraham Heschel, one of the best Jewish interpreters of the prophets, says, "God is raging in the prophet's words. . . . It is a thought staggering and hardly compatible with any rational approach to the understanding of God, that the Creator of heaven and earth should care about how an obscure individual man behaves toward poor widows and orphans." Yet God does, and the prophets bear out that concern.

Psalms gave a chance for individual poets to express their innermost thoughts and feelings to God. In the prophets, God talks back, using the same wrought-up style. The cool philosophical tone of Ecclesiastes gives way to passion as God expresses an intimate relationship with his people. In response, the prophets treat God with shocking familiarity, as if God were sitting in a chair beside them. Forgive me if this analogy seems irreverent, but in reading the prophets, I cannot help envisioning a counselor with God as a client. The counselor gets out one stock sentence, "Tell me how you really feel," and then God takes over.

I'll tell you how I feel! I feel like a parent who finds a baby girl lying in a ditch, near death. I take the girl home and make her my daughter. I clean her, pay for her schooling, feed her. I dote on her, clothe her, hang jewelry on her. Then one day she runs away. I hear reports of her life of debauchery. She's a drug addict somewhere, covered with tattoos, her body pierced with jewelry.

When my name comes up, she curses me. I feel like she's twisting a knife in my stomach.

I'll tell you how I feel! I feel like a man who falls in love with the most beautiful, sensitive woman in the world. I find her thin and wasted, abused, but I bring her home to heal her and make her beauty shine. She is the apple of my eye, and I lavish gifts and love on her. All this, and yet she forsakes me. She pants after my best friends, my enemies—anyone. She stands on a boulevard and pays people to have sex with her; unlike a common prostitute, she doesn't even charge for her services! I feel betrayed, abandoned, jilted.

God uses these examples and many others, all told with striking candor, to express his sense of betrayal over the broken covenant with Israel and all humanity. How does God really feel? Listen to his own words in Isaiah 42:

> For a long time I have kept silent,
>   I have been quiet and held myself back.
> But now, like a woman in childbirth,
>   I cry out, I gasp and pant.

One who reads the prophets encounters not an impassible, distant deity but an actual Person, a God as passionate as any person you have met. God feels delight, and frustration, and anger. He weeps and moans with pain. Again and again God is shocked by the behavior of human beings—idolatry, sexual orgies, child sacrifice—behavior that, God says, "I did not command or mention, nor did it enter my mind."

The main message expressed by the prophets boils down to this: God loves human beings. Before the prophets, you must look closely in the Old Testament to find a few scant references to God's delight or pleasure in people. The prophets proclaim loud and clear how God feels: he loves us. Of the ancient gods, Israel's God alone stooped to admit love for the flawed, two-legged creatures who roam this planet. God's cries of pain and anger are the cries of a wounded lover, distressed over our lack of response.

In the prophets God announces punishment with grief and sadness, out of a broken heart. It hurts God too, just as it hurts a human parent to punish a child. "What else can I do?" an omnipotent God asks at one point (Jeremiah 9). As he explains through Isaiah, he has no choice: if a world refuses to learn righteousness through grace, he must resort to punishment.

After every national tragedy—invasions by Assyria, Babylon, Persia—Israel has nowhere else to fall than back in the arms of God's creative love. Each time, God promises to begin again: to restore the remnant, to write laws on their hearts, to send a Messiah-deliverer, to breathe life into a pile of desiccated bones. Each time, God promises never to give up, always to love.

No prophet expresses this message more clearly than Hosea. In the very act of delivering a series of threats, God seems to break down, and a cry of love escapes:

How can I give you up, Ephraim?
    How can I hand you over, Israel? . . .
My heart is changed within me;
    all my compassion is aroused.

As if words are not strong enough to express those emotions, God asks Hosea to act out a shocking parable. Only by living out this drama could Hosea understand, and then relate to others, something of how Israel's rebuke felt to God. Hosea marries a woman named Gomer who bears him three children, then leaves Hosea for another man. She works as a prostitute, and then God gives Hosea this jarring command, "Go, show your love to your wife again, though she is loved by another and is an adulteress. Love her as the Lord loves the Israelites, though they turn to other gods. . . ." At the heart of the prophets is a God who deliberately surrenders to the wild, irresistible power of love.

As Abraham Heschel says, "Impressive as is the thought that God is too sublime to be affected by events on this insignificant planet, it stems from a line of reasoning about God derived from abstraction"—and definitely not a line of reasoning derived from the prophets. As I studied them, and absorbed their passionate intensity, I came to realize how mistaken my early impressions had been. Those who have a fixation for prophecy-as-prediction, who read these seventeen books mainly to find out what will happen after A.D. 2000, may easily miss their greatest contribution.

Why read the prophets? There is one compelling reason: to get to know God. The prophets are the Bible's most forceful revelation of God's personality.

Problem Books

Despite my new-found enthusiasm for reading the prophets, I would be remiss if I did not admit to some problems. The prophets are difficult books, more difficult than any other part of the Bible. The three complaints my friend lodged against them—"weird, confusing, and all sound alike"—do not easily disappear.

As for weirdness, eventually I came to appreciate the prophets for that very quality. I like Monty Python's comedies and Flannery O'Connor's tragedies, and whenever I mention my favorite movies, other people look at me as if I had made some social *faux pas*. As O'Connor once said in defense of her fiction: "To the hard of hearing you shout, and for the almost-blind you draw large and startling figures."

The prophets drew very startling figures indeed, and the more I studied them the more I liked them. Urbane Isaiah walked around stripped and barefoot for three years to make a political statement (imagine how the Washington press corps would treat such a protest today); Jeremiah staggered under an ox yoke to draw attention to his message of doom; Ezekiel lay on his side for months at a time, bound by ropes, facing a clay model of Jerusalem. In these ways, the prophets conveyed something too strong to be reduced to words. Weird? When a tornado is snaking directly toward your neighborhood, you don't deliver polished speeches: you jump up and down and scream like a madman.

Another complaint, "they all sound alike," soon fell by the wayside as well. Think of the three longest prophetic books: Isaiah, Jeremiah, and Ezekiel. In just a few sentences I can now identify which of the three a quote is lifted from. Isaiah writes eloquent, soaring prose; Jeremiah weeps and bleeds all over the page; Ezekiel—well, no one else's writings could be mistaken for that strange man's. (Orthodox rabbis still forbid anyone under the age of thirty to read the first three chapters of Ezekiel.)

The criticism of sameness, I concluded, comes from someone who has not really read the prophets, for they constitute a motley crew indeed. True, the prophets delivered a similar message, but each in a distinctive style. Obadiah compressed his prophecy into one sheet while a complete scroll of Isaiah stretched out for twenty-four feet. Amos was a peasant; Isaiah worked for one king and was killed by another; Daniel prospered under two different pagan empires; Jonah preferred drowning to prophesying; Zechariah's visions made Ezekiel's seem tame.

The one legitimate criticism my friend made is that the prophets are confusing. No argument. Their style of composition accounts for some of the confusion. In many cases, the prophets were not composed as books at all. Rather, they consist of speeches delivered over many years and later gathered into a collection, with few clues as to context. They thus abound with repetitions, shifts of mood, and strange images that somehow meant something to the original audience. Even Martin Luther admitted they "have a queer way of talking, like people who, instead of proceeding in an orderly manner, ramble off from one thing to the next, so that you cannot make head or tail of them or see what they are getting at."

Must one pore over commentaries for years in order to understand these books? Is there any way for the average person to wend through the labyrinth? I have learned a few clues that help me see beyond the arcana to the essential message of the prophets. I present them because they have helped me overcome barriers to reading the prophets, especially barriers that lingered from the prediction-fixation of my childhood church.

Now and Later

Sometimes we act as if the prophets lived primarily for the benefit of people not yet born—like us. The very word "prophet" has come to mean a teller of the future, a form of crystal-ball gazer. I wish we could scrap that word "prophet" and replace it with "seer," which better conveys their role: to see what no one else can, with an X-ray vision into the present and the future. Prophets simply see better than anyone else.

It becomes clear as you read the prophets that *now* was more important to them than *later.* I roughly divide the prophets' insights into three categories:

1. *Now:* prophecies that relate primarily to the prophet's own day (Assyria will invade Moab; Israel's alliance with Egypt will backfire).
2. *Later:* predictions of future events well removed from the prophet's own time but later fulfilled in history (for example, the many Messianic prophecies that New Testament authors apply to Jesus Christ).

3. *Much Later:* prophecies that seem still to lie in the
future (which may include references to a time of
worldwide tribulation and a future mass conversion of
the Jews, though scholars disagree on the precise meaning of almost all such references).

A most confusing aspect of the prophets is that they do not
bother telling us whether the predicted events—invasions,
earthquakes, a coming Leader, a recreated earth—will occur the
next day, a thousand years later, or three thousand years later.
In fact, near and distant predictions often appear in the same
paragraph, blurring together. Read Isaiah 13, for example, and
you will think the overthrow of Babylon by the Persians will
usher in the end of the world. (Probably the prophets did not
know a timetable—after all, Jesus admitted ignorance of God's
schedule while he lived on earth.)

Or consider Joel 2, which describes the devastation caused
by an army of locusts. Nearly everyone assumes Joel was referring to an actual insect plague during his own time—the period
I have called Now. But the same chapter speaks of a time when
the Spirit will be poured out on all people, and sons and daughters will prophesy. Clearly, that passage refers to a Later event,
the time just after Pentecost, for the apostle Peter says as much
in his sermon in Acts 2. But what of this verse in the middle of
the same paragraph: "The sun will be turned to darkness and
the moon to blood before the coming of the great and dreadful
day of the Lord"? Joel is using metaphorical language, of course,
but he goes on to describe a gathering of all nations for a final
judgment (Much Later?), and then shifts back to a discussion of
Tyre and Sidon, two of Israel's contemporary neighbors.

To complicate matters, sometimes the prophets describe an
event that apparently has two different fulfillments, one Now
and one Later. Isaiah's famous prophecy "The virgin will be with
child and will give birth to a son, and will call him Immanuel"
(7:14) fits this category. The next two verses make clear that the

sign had a fulfillment in Isaiah's own day (many scholars assume the child to be Isaiah's own), and yet Matthew links the prophecy's final fulfillment to the Virgin Mary.

Biblical scholars have names for this characteristic of the prophets: double or triple fulfillment, part-for-the-whole, creative bisociation. Naturally, such complicated devices raise questions. How are we to know whether a prophet is describing something in his own day (Now) or something unfulfilled (Later or Much Later) or both? The prophets' creations bring to mind an American primitive painting that has no visual clues of perspective, its houses, mountains, trees, animals, and farmers all compressed into the same dimension. To interpret the scene, the viewer must separate these various elements and reconstruct them in a way that makes visual sense.

I believe this prophetic device, admittedly confusing, offers a glimpse into how God views history. As "seers," the prophets have insight into God's perspective, and for a God who lives outside the constraints of time, sequence is a minor issue. The lamb, says the apostle Peter, "was chosen before the creation of the world, but was revealed in these last times for your sake" (1 Peter 1:20). Paul added that God also chose his followers "before the creation of the world" (Ephesians 1:4). Similarly, our hope of eternal life was promised "before the beginning of time" (Titus 1:2). Long before Einstein's theory of the relativity of time and space, the New Testament writers established some truths as, quite literally, timeless. God, a timeless reality, enters our time-bound history as an artist would enter his own painting, suggests C. S. Lewis.

Should it surprise us that incursions into time by a timeless being would have overtones that reverberate in Isaiah's day, and Mary's, and also our own? The prophesied birth of a child during the reign of King Ahaz confirmed Isaiah's predictive ability and thus gave evidence that Isaiah's other, exalted prophecies of "Wonderful Counselor, Mighty God, Everlasting Father,

Prince of Peace" would come to pass. Isaiah did not give a time frame for the final fulfillment of his prophecies, for in all probability he did not even understand such a time frame.

The Hebrew prophets spoke to a world spinning out of control. Israel was shrinking, surrounded on all sides by tyrannical powers, and God seemed silent, hidden, even powerless. The prophets project forward in time to a period when God will break his silence. In that day, they tell us, God will move in forcefully to recreate heaven and earth. He will swallow up death and dry all tears. There will be no more poverty, no hunger, no violence. A banquet feast will be spread for one and all. Then we will know God face to face, and all earth will serve him.

Almost all predictions, however, had meaning for the original hearers as well as for us thousands of years later. The prophets told of a recreated heaven and earth in order to demonstrate that history would be determined by the future— God's future—and not by the present reality of suffering, chaos, and political upheaval. But in order to believe in such a lofty vision, that audience needed temporal evidence: events being worked out on schedule, according to prediction, in their own time, in the Now. Hence the predictions that found fulfillment in the prophets' own lifetimes.

Christopher J. H. Wright offers an analogy that helps explain why later generations were so dense at recognizing the later fulfillment of prophecies (remember, the Jewish scribes all missed the prophecies about Jesus of Nazareth). Imagine a five-year-old son in, say, 1900 whose father promises him a horse for his twenty-first birthday. Would such a boy be disappointed if instead in 1916 he receives a model-T Ford?

> It would be a strange son who would accuse his father of breaking his promise just because there was no horse. And even stranger if, in spite of having received the far superior motor car, the son insisted that the promise would only be fulfilled if a horse *also* materialized, since

that was the literal promise. It is obvious that with the change in circumstances, unknown at the time the promise was made, the father has more than kept his promise. In fact he has done so in a way that *surpasses* the original words of the promise that were necessarily limited by the mode of transport available at that time. The promise was made in terms understood at the time. It was fulfilled in the light of new historical events.

—*Knowing Jesus Through the Old Testament*

Indeed, for this very reason, prophecy paradoxically works best in reverse. A New Testament writer such as Matthew or Paul could look back and demonstrate how Jesus fulfilled the terms of the Jewish covenant and the predictions of the prophets, even though most people in Jesus' own day failed to make the connection. Jesus' contemporaries were looking for a new King David to rule over Jerusalem; God sent instead a Servant King to rule over the entire universe. The author of Hebrews underscores how the fulfillment surpassed the promise:

In the past God spoke to our forefathers through the prophets at many times and in various ways, but in these last days he has spoken to us by his Son, whom he appointed heir of all things, and through whom he made the universe. The Son is the radiance of God's glory and the exact representation of his being, sustaining all things by his powerful word.

For this same reason we should approach a book like Revelation with cautious humility. John wrote in terms applicable in his day (horsemen, the harlot Babylon, streets of gold) but no one knows for certain how those prophecies will find fulfillment. We can safely assume, though, that God will fulfill them in a way that *surpasses* the original promise.

My own reading gradually changed as I began to see how the prophets themselves emphasized a flow in the reverse direction, from Later to Now. They defined human longing—

every utopian vision traces back to their wonderful words—and portrayed a glorious future in order to affect Now behavior. They offered a vision of the World as God Wants It for people to cling to even in a time of turmoil and despair.

Formerly, I had turned to the prophets for clues into the future, the Later and Much Later. Will the world end in a nuclear holocaust? Does global warming herald the last days? Rather, their message should primarily be affecting my Now. Do I trust in a loving, powerful God even in our chaotic century? Do I cling to God's vision of peace and justice even when the Church is often identified with war and oppression? Do I believe that God reigns, though this world shows little evidence of it?

Instinctively, we want to fly to the future. The prophets point us back to the present, yet ask us to live in the light of the future they image up. Can we trust their vision and accept it as the true reality of earth, despite all evidence to the contrary? Can we live Now "as if" God is loving, gracious, merciful, and all-powerful? The prophets remind us that indeed God is and that history itself will one day bear that out. The World as It Is will become the World as God Wants It.

Kathleen Norris, who lives in the farm country of South Dakota, speaks of "next-year-country," a landscape farmers know well: *next year the rains will come, next year hail won't fall, next year winter will hold off a few weeks.* Yet, continues Norris, she doesn't know a single farmer who uses the idea of "next year" as an excuse not to get out and do the work needed now. She adds that maybe we ought to use prophetic literature in the same way: "not as an allowance to indulge in an otherworldly fixation but as an injunction to pay closer attention to the world around us."

> The apocalypticists asked about the kingdom of God, the absolute future, in the light of the present situation of man and the world. That is why they were so concerned about the exact date of its arrival. Jesus takes the very opposite line: he asks about the present situation of man and the

world in the light of the imminent advent of God's future kingdom. That is why he is not concerned about the time or manner of the arrival of God's kingdom.

—Hans Küng, *On Being a Christian*

God's Point of View

The mixed-together time sequence—Now/Later/Much Later— hints at what I consider to be the chief contribution of the prophets: they render God's point of view. God granted them (and, through them, us) the extraordinary vision to see past this world, dominated as it is by great powers and larger-than-life tyrants, to a different level of reality. We get a glimpse, a mere glimpse, of history from God's viewpoint. No wonder the prophets seem strange: we lack the capacity for seeing the world from the vantage point of timelessness.

Studying the prophets is like staring at one of the multi-dimensional "stereogram" artworks in vogue on the West Coast. At first you see a pleasing pattern of lines and swirls, but if you keep staring at that pattern for four or five minutes suddenly another scene emerges, this one a school of whales, latent but hidden in the original maze of lines. It stands out so strongly, in fact, that you have trouble getting your eyes to reconstruct the original pattern.

I detect in the prophets at least three levels of meaning, a kind of trifocal vision. Sometimes the prophets describe current events in the same style a daily newspaper would use: "The Philistines are amassing troops in the North ... A huge swarm of locusts is approaching our southern borders ... Damascus is rumored to be joining a conspiracy against Assyria." Portions of the prophets (Isaiah 36–39, for example) quote directly from historical books and record the day's events in matter-of-fact prose.

Rarely did the prophets stop there, however. Much like medieval minstrels who composed ballads to give meaning to each day's events, the prophets interpreted the newspaper view of the world from a moral perspective. They saw military invasions and locust plagues not merely as natural occurrences, rather as judgments of God. Such disasters inevitably follow when people exploit the poor, trample the weak, and turn their backs on God.

This second level of vision should not surprise us, for modern-day prophets do the same thing. Often quoting the biblical prophets in his writings, Martin Luther King Jr. pointed to the moral dimensions of the Civil Rights Movement; for him, defeating racism was a spiritual crusade, not just a political issue. In city after city around the world, Billy Graham has interpreted the disruptions in modern civilization as evidence of a spiritual decline. Alexander Solzhenitsyn pronounced the compound tragedies of twentieth-century Russia as a consequence of a society who forgot God. Even secular historians do something similar. When a race riot breaks out, they hark back to the underlying moral causes: a history of slavery, poverty in the inner city, the breakdown of families.

According to Abraham Heschel, ancient society cherished three things above all else: wisdom, wealth, and might. (Has anything changed since then?) The Hebrew prophets blasted all three of these values, any of which could become idols. None provides the kind of foundation a society needs; only trust in the living God can do that. This moral view of history differs markedly from the newspaper view, which tends to focus on fame and power—tokens of the very wisdom, wealth, and might that the prophets denounced.

In Isaiah's day, for example, tyrants such as Sennacherib and Sargon of Assyria dominated the headlines, and it surely seemed that history revolved around them. When Assyrian armies steamrolled through Judah, everyone in the country cowered in fear—everyone except Isaiah, that is. With prescient moral vision, he scorned the Assyrian rulers as bit players, temporary tools that

God would use and then toss aside. With biting satire, Isaiah passed moral judgment on all great political rulers. Isaiah 14 should be chiseled over the gravestone of every tyrant in history, from Sennacherib to Nebuchadnezzar to Hitler and Stalin and Pol Pot. It depicts long-dead rulers rising from the grave to greet the new ones: "You also have become weak, as we are; you have become like us," they say; "Maggots are spread out beneath you and worms cover you." Eventually, all tyrants meet the same fate: "Is this the man who shook the earth and made kingdoms tremble?" people will ask. Isaiah urged his people to put their faith in God alone.

Prophets like Isaiah had no more courage than ordinary people—their arguments with God prove that—but they did have a special vision, an in-sight into the "God within the shadows." That vision cast history in a different light. Who is really running the world? the Hebrew prophets asked. King Ahab or God? The Assyrian empire or God? (Or, we might add, the U.S. Congress or God?) With no weapon other than the sheer moral force of the spoken word, they stood against the powers of their day. One of the great vindications of the prophets is that their predictions, which seemed preposterous at the time, proved true. What did pipsqueak Hebrews know about the intricacies of power politics? A lot, as it turned out: Assyria fell, as did Babylon, mighty Babylon, and eventually Persia, Greece, and ultimately even Rome.

Today, archeologists in Iraq must dig through layers of dirt to find any remnants of Babylonian culture. Nebuchadnezzar is a mere footnote of history. Yet the prophecies of Jeremiah and Daniel have been preserved and are still studied by millions around the world. And if the messages concerning Moab and Philistia and Assyria and Babylon proved true in precise detail, then what of their message about the end of all history?

Cosmic Combat

Occasionally the prophets add yet a third point of view to their newspaper and moral interpretations of the world: they pull aside a screen and permit a glimpse into the cosmic view of history. Like John Milton in *Paradise Lost,* or Goethe in *Faust,* the prophets portray this world as a stage on which individual people are acting, albeit under the influence of unseen forces offstage. Job presents the Old Testament's purest sketch of this cosmic point of view, and the prophets, as "seers" with powers of vision unavailable to others, give further glimpses.

Zechariah and Ezekiel had numerous visions into the history behind history, and recorded them in scenes that have baffled scholars ever since. Daniel got a lesson about the cosmic point of view (chapter 10) when an angel explained that "the prince of the Persian kingdom" had prevented him from answering Daniel's prayer for twenty-one days. Finally, after a three-week standoff, reinforcements arrived, and Michael, one of the chief angels, helped him break through the opposition. Like Job, Daniel played a decisive role in the warfare between cosmic forces of good and evil, though much of the action took place beyond his range of vision.

Revelation, the New Testament's only book majoring on prophecy, offers the most vivid examples of the cosmic point of view. Consider Revelation 12, which surely ranks as one of the strangest chapters in the Bible. It tells of a pregnant woman clothed with the sun, an enormous seven-headed red dragon whose tail sweeps a third of the stars from the sky, a flight into the desert, and a war in heaven. If you scour the commentaries, you'll find as many interpretations of this chapter as you will commentators, but almost all of them say it has something to do with the Incarnation, Mary and Joseph's flight from Herod into Egypt, and the amplified effect of Jesus' birth on the entire universe.

In a sense, Revelation 12 presents the other side of Christmas, adding a new set of holographic images to the familiar scenes of manger and shepherds and the Slaughter of the Innocents. What happened on earth, and is recorded in Matthew and Luke, represented ripples on the surface; underneath, massive disruptions were shaking the foundations of the universe. From God's viewpoint—and Satan's—Christmas signals far more than the birth of a baby; it was an invasion, the decisive advance in the great struggle for the cosmos.

Which is the true picture of Christmas, the account in the Gospels or that in Revelation? Is the enormous red dragon to be understood literally or "just" as a figure of speech? The phrasing itself gives us away. As C. S. Lewis and others remind us, mythic images serve as powerful carriers of truth. When God really wanted to get through to his prophets, he gave them access to a cosmic point of view rich in mythic images.

Would it be too strong to say that the cosmic point of view most resembles the way God himself sees history? Let me explain. Most of us prefer a more literal, newspaper view. When we encounter cosmic images, such as in Revelation, we immediately try to explain them, to transpose them into our own vocabulary of history. That is why the prophecy conference speakers drape bed sheets across the platform and explain Daniel's visions in terms of Jerusalem and China and the European Union and maybe even Saddam Hussein. When furnished a glimpse of the cosmic point of view, we tend to translate it downward.

Nevertheless, as the prophets tell us, the vicissitudes of history that so engage us—military alliances, who gets elected, the rise and fall of kingdoms—are merely the stage on which the real battle is being played out. The significant questions are not "How much territory does Nebuchadnezzar (or Russia or China) control?" but rather, "Is the kingdom of God advancing? Are God's people remaining faithful? Do we believe that God reigns?"

When a baby was born, the universe shuddered. When seventy-two disciples went on a short-term mission assignment (Luke 10), Satan fell like lightning from heaven. What happens here on earth affects the future of the cosmos. From God's point of view, the future has already been determined, and the prophets spell out that future state in glowing detail: swords beaten into plowshares, a lamb recumbent beside a lion, a banquet feast. That is what God wants for this earth and that is what God will accomplish on this earth. The end is settled. What remains is whether we will live believing it.

What Difference?

Richard Foster repeats an old Jewish story about a little boy who went to a prophet and said, "Prophet, don't you see? You have been prophesying now for fifteen years, and things are still the same. Why do you keep on?" And the prophet said, "Don't you know, little boy, I'm not prophesying to change the world, but to prevent the world from changing me."

We cannot fully comprehend the cosmic point of view, and at times we all find ourselves overwhelmed by the crushing contradictions in our world. Like Job, like the psalmists, like Habakkuk and Jeremiah, we question God's wisdom or his power or his love. Bound in time, we see history second by second, minute by minute, hour by hour. The prophets call us beyond the fears and grim reality of present history to the view of all eternity, to a time when God's reign will fill the earth with light and truth. That is what Habakkuk meant by his famous phrase, "The just shall live by faith": we cling to belief in God's goodness even in a world falling apart.

In a word, the prophets offer us hope. In *The House of the Dead*, Dostoevsky tells of an orthodox Jew who faithfully carried out his religious duties in the midst of a Russian prison. He covered a table in the corner of the cell, opened a book, lighted candles, fastened leather bracelets on his arms and forehead, and began to pray. As he read from the sacred book, he would suddenly cover his head with both hands and sob. All at once, to the astonishment of anyone who was watching for the first time, he would break off his sobs, burst into a laugh, and recite a hymn of triumph. When asked about his strange performance, the Jew replied that his sobs and tears were provoked by the destruction of Jerusalem. The law required him to groan and strike his breast. At the moment of the most acute grief, however, he was to remember a prophecy that the Jews would one day return to Jerusalem, and this sent him into a state of uncontrolled joy. Hope chased away every other emotion.

What difference do ancient prophetic visions make to those of us stuck in this fallen world? They awaken in us what we hope to be ultimately true. Would it make a difference for blacks in urban America, or Christians in Muslim prisons, to know how God feels about their plight? Did it matter to the slaves in the American South to believe that God was not satisfied with a world that included masters armed with bullwhips and lynching ropes? Would it make a difference for any of us to know that God is indeed a God of justice and peace and hope, no matter how this world appears?

The prophets call us to a vision of a deeper, underlying reality, to "joy beyond the walls of the world, more poignant than grief" (Tolkien's phrase). By giving a glimpse of the future, and of the cosmic present, they make it possible for us to believe in a just God after all. Justice is essential to the prophets, for God's reputation rides on whether he can ultimately deliver justice to this world. Like a bell tolling from another world, the prophets proclaim that no matter how things now appear, there is no future in evil, only in good.

When you live, time-bound, in a world like ours, it takes faith to believe God's view of history as presented in Isaiah 25 and 65 or Revelation 21–22. Faith, according to Hebrews 11, consists in "being sure of what we hope for and certain of what we do not see." The faithful ones described in that great chapter did not receive the things promised in their lifetimes (v. 13), and I identify with those men and women because neither in my lifetime do I see many swords being melted into plowshares. Death, with all its ugly new mutations of AIDS and environmental cancers, is still swallowing people up, not being swallowed. Evil, not good, appears to be winning.

In strange, complex images, the prophets present a wholly different view of the world. They offer hope, and something else: a challenge for us to live out the World as God Wants It in this life, right now. In settlements of God's kingdom, we can participate in the great struggle that will someday usher in a new heaven and new earth.

We may never figure out the toes and horns of Daniel's beasts, or the intricacies of Revelation 12. But if only we could believe that our struggle really is against principalities and powers, if only we could believe that God will prove himself trustworthy and set right all that is wrong, if only we could demonstrate God's passion for justice and truth in this world—then, I think, the prophets will have accomplished their most urgent mission.

I confess that, despite long hours of study in the prophets, I have no clearer understanding of what will happen next year, or in 2025. But I have a much clearer idea of what God wants to accomplish in my life right now. And I am gaining, gradually, the confidence to believe in the present what will fully make sense only when seen from the future.

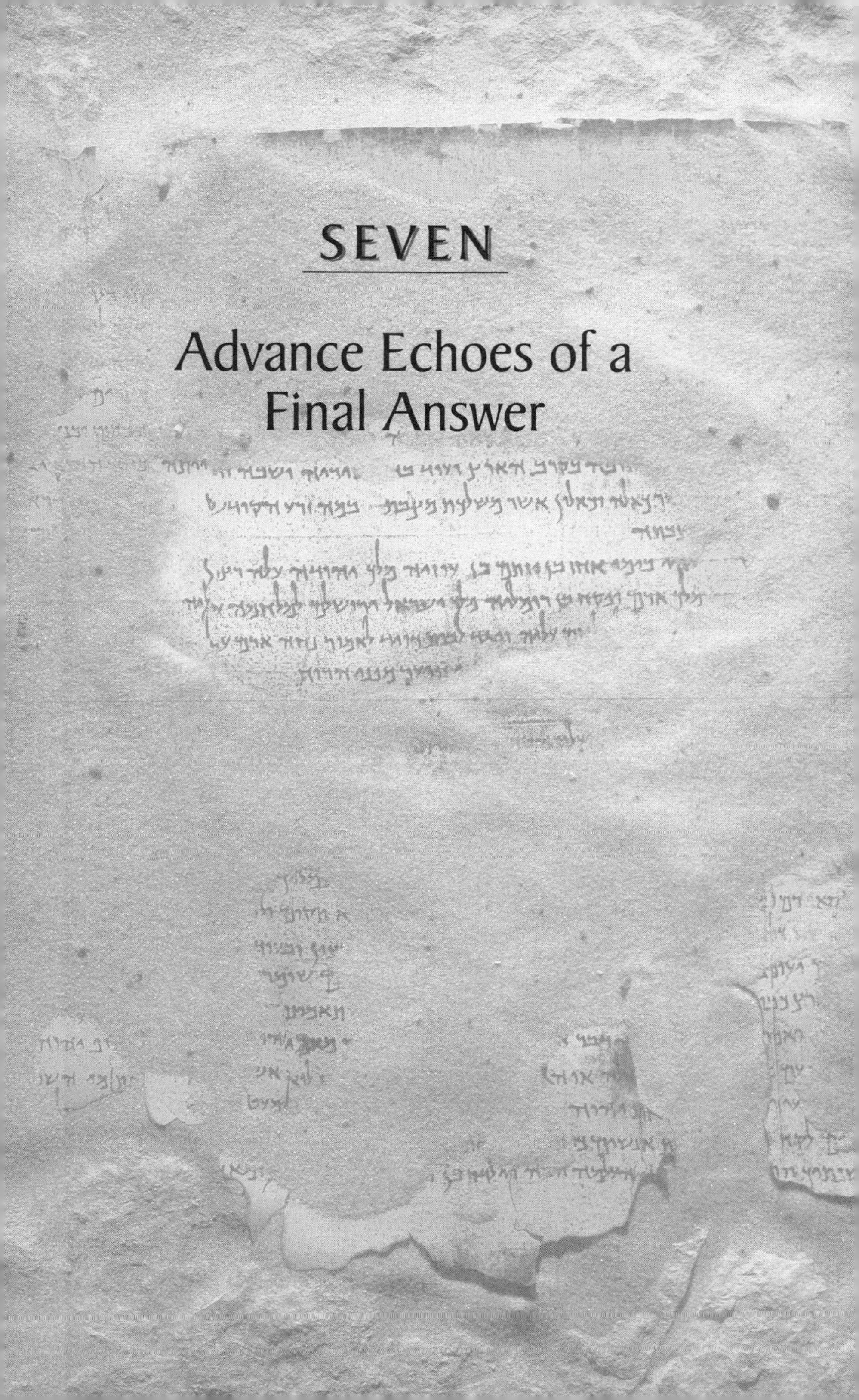

SEVEN

Advance Echoes of a Final Answer

SEVEN

Advance Echoes of a Final Answer

*The earth trembles under the foot of Jesus Christ. The ferret has
been put into the warren.*

—Paul Claudel

I remember driving through rural Georgia, my home state, in
the late 1960s. This was the Deep South, where religion is as
ubiquitous as fried food and high school football, and occasionally I saw on a highway bridge or railroad trestle a zealot's
hand-painted advertisement for God: "Jesus is coming soon—
are you ready?" or "Prepare to meet thy God." The smart-alecky
spirit of the decade, however, had even infiltrated the Bible
Belt. On a large boulder beneath the stately phrase "Jesus is the
answer," someone had scrawled, "So what's the question?"

That roadside dialogue stuck with me, and I later saw it
making an appearance on placards and bumper stickers. The
graffitist may have intended little more than an irreverent joke,
but he or she had in fact identified the crux of Christian apologetics. Why follow Jesus unless he answers some inner longing
that nothing else can satisfy?

I have learned to love the Old Testament because it so
poignantly expresses my own inner longings. I find in it a realism about human nature that is sorely absent from much smiley-
face Christian propaganda. And yet the Old Testament writers,

especially the psalmists and prophets, eagerly point ahead to a time when God has vowed to address those longings, to answer the questions that never go away. Those anguished questions, promise the writers, will find at least partial resolution when Messiah arrives.

Deuteronomy prefigures the failure of God's covenant with his people, spelling out in frightening detail what will happen when the Hebrews turn their back on God. The prophets' doleful refrains to Moses' swan song underscore that failure. Not just the nation fails; every individual fails to keep the covenant. The wisdom books, especially Ecclesiastes, demonstrate beyond all doubt the impotence of knowledge, wealth, and genes to change basic human character. Thus the Old Testament ends with the gap between God and human beings as wide as ever.

When I wrote a book about Jesus (*The Jesus I Never Knew*) I was struck by how meticulously Jesus connected himself to the Old Testament. "Do not think that I have come to abolish the Law or the Prophets; I have not come to abolish them but to fulfill them," he said in the Sermon on the Mount. He chided devout Jewish detractors, "You diligently study the Scriptures because you think that by them you possess eternal life. These are the Scriptures that testify about me, yet you refuse to come to me to have life." And on the road to Emmaus after his resurrection he said, "This is what I told you while I was still with you: Everything must be fulfilled that is written about me in the Law of Moses, the Prophets and the Psalms." To borrow a phrase from H. Richard Niebuhr, Jesus is the Rosetta stone of faith whose existence explains all that goes before.

The Old Testament tells a story about Creation and the Fall, then God's painstaking effort to construct a nation out of the rubble of human failure. The New Testament keeps the basic plot intact but reinterprets the point of the story. It identifies Jesus as the "seed of the woman" promised in the Garden of

Eden and then connects him to other central characters: the "Second Adam," the "Son of Abraham," the "Son of David."

In a sense, all of Old Testament history serves as a preparation for Jesus, with the characters on its pages contributing a family, an identity, and a race for Jesus to be born into. What did God have in mind with the long, convoluted story of the Hebrews? The answer of the New Testament is unequivocal: Jesus is what God had in mind. He came to reconcile humanity to God by extending God's kingdom beyond the boundaries of race to the entire world.

"Of the whole of Scripture there are two parts: the law and the gospel," said Philip Melanchthon. "The law indicates the sickness, the gospel the remedy." Which brings me back to the graffiti scrawled on the rock in Georgia: What exactly does Jesus remedy? To what questions does Jesus provide the answer for me? Am I hanging on to faith out of habit, like a regional accent I grew up with and can't seem to shed? Or does Jesus indeed provide the answer to some fundamental question of my existence? Unless he does, I may as well convert to Judaism and read the Old Testament exclusively.

As I think back over the Old Testament, especially the portions I have discussed in this book, three questions keep resurfacing in different forms—the same three questions that attract most of my own doubts. I return again and again to the Old Testament because it faces head-on these very questions. Do I matter? Does God care? Why doesn't God act? These are the watersheds of my faith. If Jesus is the answer for me, then he must somehow speak to these three questions.

Do I Matter?

I stand in the cashier line of the local supermarket and look around me. I see teenagers with shaved heads and nose rings, picking through the snack foods; a Yuppie buying one steak, a few twigs of asparagus, and a baked potato; an elderly woman hunched over from osteoporosis, squeezing bruises into the peaches and strawberries. Does God know all these people by name? I ask myself. Do they really matter to him?

Sometimes when I watch the scenes of abortion protests and counter-protests on the evening news, I try to envision the unborns who are prompting such ferocity. I have seen fetuses on display in museum jars to illustrate the progressive stages of human development. Worldwide, about six million of these tiny fetuses are disposed of each year—*murdered*, say the protestors. The image of God rests inside each one, say the theologians. What does God think of six million human beings who die never having seen the outside of a uterus? I wonder. Do they matter to him?

What I know about astronomy also feeds my doubt. Scientists tell us that our sun is one of perhaps 500 billion stars in the Milky Way, a medium-sized galaxy among two hundred billion others, all swarming with stars. Can one person on a speck of a planet in a speck of a solar system in a mediocre clump of a galaxy really make a difference to the Creator of that Universe?

"When I consider your heavens," said a star-gazing psalmist who must have shared my point of view, "what is man that you are mindful of him?" Every Old Testament book I have considered circles around this question. Toiling in Egypt, the Hebrew slaves could hardly believe Moses' assurances that God would concern himself with their plight. Job's friends mocked the absurd notion that puny Job mattered to the Lord of the Universe. The Teacher in Ecclesiastes would have phrased the question more cynically: Does *anything* really matter under the sun? Isn't all of life meaningless?

I was entertaining such doubts myself several years ago when a letter came inviting me to address a Christian conference in New England. The invitation letter gave the theme for the conference, a verse from Isaiah 49: "Behold, I have engraved you on the palms of my hands." I had to smile at the irony of timing. In my frame of mind, I hardly felt equipped to comfort the saints of New England with the kind of verse that is often embroidered and hung on walls as a plaque of faith. I considered turning down the invitation or asking if I might speak on some other theme. Before doing so, however, I opened the book of Isaiah and read the context of that verse.

I discovered that God made this stirring declaration to people suffering through perhaps the lowest point in the entire Old Testament. Israel had been annihilated, its holy city of Jerusalem profaned. Babylonian soldiers met no resistance as they entered the temple's inner sanctum; this time, God did not rescue his people. Their temple desecrated, their capital city razed, the Hebrews were shipped in chains to Babylon (the site of present-day Iraq).

Psalm 137 expresses how it felt to be one of God's people then:

> By the rivers of Babylon we sat and wept. . . .
> If I forget you, O Jerusalem,
>   may my right hand forget its skill.
> May my tongue cling to the roof of my mouth
>   if I do not remember you. . . .
> O Daughter of Babylon, doomed to destruction,
>   happy is he who repays you
>   for what you have done to us—
> he who seizes your infants
>   and dashes them against the rocks.

It suddenly dawned on me that the Hebrews in Babylon who received the message of Isaiah 49 were agonizing over the very same question I had been asking. *Do we matter to God?* This is what it means to be the chosen people—to have our land plowed under, our cities razed, our women and children murdered, our strong men sent into exile? Similar questions have been asked by Anabaptists, Huguenots, Armenians, Russian

Pentecostals, Palestinian Christians, Sudanese, and other suffering believers through the centuries.

"The Lord has forsaken me, the Lord has forgotten me," the Hebrews lament during this time of crisis (Isaiah 49:14), and it is to these people that God makes a vow. "Can a mother forget the baby at her breast?" God asks rhetorically. "Though she may forget, I will not forget you! See, I have engraved you on the palms of my hands."

At this bleak moment, the nadir of the Old Covenant, God gives a series of promises in direct response to the questions tormenting the Hebrews. Bible scholars call them the Servant Songs, and they appear tucked into Isaiah 42–53. They are at once gorgeous poetry and essential prophecy, some of the most explicit prophecies we have. Taken together, the Servant Songs set the stage for the Messiah, God's answer to the Hebrews' question.

In effect, God puts his reputation on the line. He will answer the Hebrews' bitter complaint with an act of boldness, imagination, and courage that none of them could have dreamed of, an event that will test the limits of human credibility and divine humiliation. God agrees to join them on planet Earth, "to write himself on the pages of history," in Jacques Ellul's words. The mysterious Servant Songs of Isaiah plainly foretell the Incarnation (as the New Testament points out at least ten times).

The Jews, raised on volcanic images of Sinai, with a reverence for God so profound that they would neither speak nor write his name, would ever wait in fear, not just hope, for the coming of Messiah. "But who can endure the day of his coming?" cried the prophet Malachi in alarm, "For he will be like a refiner's fire." If the Lord of Hosts paid a personal visit to corrupted Earth, would any of its inhabitants survive? Would Earth itself survive?

Yet, as Isaiah makes clear, the God who visits Earth comes not in a raging whirlwind, nor in a devouring fire. "Behold, a virgin shall conceive and bear a Son, and shall call his name Emmanuel, 'God with us.'" He arrives instead in the tiniest, least threatening form imaginable: as an ovum, and then fetus, growing cell by cell inside a peasant virgin. That egg divides and redivides until a fetus takes shape, and finally a single baby bursts forth from Mary's loins to join the puny human beings on their speck of a planet.

The Messiah rules, surely, but he rules with a rod of love. Who can endure the day of his coming? Anyone can endure it; all who come, he welcomes with love and gladness.

In effect, the holiday we celebrate as Christmas memorializes God's answer to the Hebrews' question, *Do we matter?* Here on earth, for thirty-three years, God experienced in flesh what it is like to be one of us. In the stories he told, and the people whose lives he touched, Jesus answered for all time that vexing question.

Jesus said God is like a shepherd who leaves ninety-nine sheep inside the fence to hunt frantically for one stray; like a father who can't stop thinking about his rebellious ingrate of a son though he has another who is respectful and obedient; like a rich host who opens the doors of the banquet hall to a menagerie of bag-ladies and bums. God loves people not as a race or species, but rather just as you and I love them: one at a time. We *matter* to God. In a rare moment when he pulled back the curtain between seen and unseen worlds, Jesus said that angels rejoice when a single sinner repents. A solitary act on this speck of a planet reverberates throughout the cosmos.

In his social contacts Jesus went out of his way to embrace the unloved and unworthy, the folks who matter little to the rest of society but matter infinitely to God. People with leprosy quarantined outside the city wall, Jesus touched, even as his disciples shrank back in disgust. A half-breed woman who had gone through five husbands already and was no doubt the center of the town's gossip industry, Jesus tapped as his first missionary.

Another woman, too full of shame over her embarrassing condition to approach Jesus face to face, grabbed his robe, hoping he would not notice. He did notice. She learned, like so many other "nobodies," that you can't easily escape Jesus' gaze. We matter too much.

Novelist Reynolds Price said there is one sentence all humankind craves to hear: "The Maker of all things loves and wants me." That is the sentence Jesus proclaimed, loud as sweet thunder. The Maker of all things is the maker of all human beings, an odd species that he, unfathomably, deemed worthy of individual attention and love. He demonstrated that love in person, on the gnarly hills of Palestine, and ultimately on a cross.

What the prophets spoke about, Jesus lived. "I have engraved you on the palms of my hands," God said in Isaiah's day. When he visited earth in the form of a Servant, he showed that the hand of God is not too big for the smallest person in the world. It is a hand engraved with our individual names and engraved also with wounds, the cost to God of loving us so much.

My doubts, I confess, resemble a disability more than a disease: they never go away completely. Now, though, when I find myself wallowing in self-pity, overwhelmed by the ache of cosmic loneliness that is articulated so well in books like Job and Ecclesiastes, I turn to the Gospel accounts of Jesus' stories and deeds. If I conclude that my existence "under the sun" makes no difference to God, I contradict one of the main reasons God came to earth. To the question, *Do I matter?* Jesus is indeed the answer.

Does God Care?

In *The Soul of the Night*, astronomer Chet Raymo tells this story:

> Yesterday on Boston Common I saw a young man on a skateboard collide with a child. The skateboarder was racing down the promenade and smashed into the child with full force. I saw this happen from a considerable dis-

tance. It happened without a sound. It happened in dead silence. The cry of the terrified child as she darted to avoid the skateboard and the scream of the child's mother at the moment of impact were absorbed by the gray wool of the November day. The child's body simply lifted up into the air and, in slow motion, as if in a dream, floated above the promenade, bounced twice like a rubber ball, and lay still.

All of this happened in perfect silence. It was as if I were watching the tragedy through a telescope. It was as if the tragedy were happening on another planet. I have seen stars exploding in space, colossal, planet-shattering, distanced by light-years, framed in the cold glass of a telescope, utterly silent. It was like that.

Raymo adds one more sentence, "How are we to understand the silence of the universe?" The question haunts the rest of his book, and he returns to it often as he tells of his loss of childhood faith. For Chet Raymo, as for so many others, God's silence in the face of earth's suffering poses a question with no answer.

The fact that I am a Christian makes Raymo's question harder for me, not easier. For a person who sees the universe as a product of chaos and randomness, what should one expect but silence? How, though, can those of us who see it as a product of God's creative love account for the silence? How can we believe that God cares?

Much of my career as a writer has revolved around the problem of pain. The book titles I choose— *Where Is God When It Hurts, Disappointment with God*—betray me. Like Chet Raymo, I return again and again to the same questions, as if fingering an old wound that never quite heals. I hear from readers of my books, and their anguished stories give human faces to my doubts.

I mentioned in another book a distressing week when two people called to talk about their experiences of disappointment with God. One, a youth pastor in Colorado, had just learned his wife and baby daughter were dying of AIDS. The mother had received a contaminated blood transfusion just before her delivery date. "How can I talk to my youth group about a loving God?" he asked me. "How can I tell them God cares?"

That same week I also heard from a blind man calling on a public phone. Several months before, he had invited a recovering drug addict into his home as an act of mercy. He had just learned the recovering addict was molesting his wife—under his own roof. "It's like God is punishing me for trying to serve him," he said. Blind, he began to imagine all that had been going on. Had the addict forced his wife, or did she cooperate willingly? Just then he ran out of quarters, and the phone went dead. Silence.

I have learned not even to attempt an answer to the "Why?" questions. Why did the youth pastor's wife happen to get the one tainted bottle of blood? Why does a tornado hit one town in Oklahoma and skip over another? Why did that one woman's child get hit by a skateboard on Boston Common? I do not know, and, frankly, after much study I have concluded the Bible does not give us the answer. In his speech to Job, when God had a golden opportunity to enlighten us on causation issues, God avoided the topic entirely.

One question, however, no longer plagues me as it once did. The question *Does God care?* lurks behind Chet Raymo's poignant story about the silent universe. It also lurks behind much of the Old Testament. Job reluctantly concluded that, no, God could not care about him or about other suffering people. "How faint the whisper we hear of him," sighed Job. The psalmists cried out for some sign that God heard their prayers, some evidence that he had not forsaken them.

I know of only one way to answer the question *Does God care?* and for me it has proved decisive: Jesus is the answer. Jesus never attempted a philosophical answer to the problem of pain, yet he did give an existential answer. Although I cannot learn from him why a particular bad thing occurs, I can learn how God feels about it. Jesus gives God a face, and that face is streaked with tears.

Whenever I read straight through the Bible, a huge difference between the Old and New Testaments comes to light. In the Old Testament I can find many expressions of doubt and disappointment. Whole books—Jeremiah, Habakkuk, Job—center on the theme. As I have said, almost half of the psalms have a dark, brooding tone about them. In striking contrast, the New Testament Epistles contain little of this type of anguish. The problem of pain has surely not gone away: James 1, Romans 5 and 8, the entire book of 1 Peter, and much of Revelation deal with the subject in detail. Nevertheless, nowhere do I find the piercing question, *Does God care?* I see nothing resembling the accusation of Psalm 77: "Has God forgotten to be merciful?"

The reason for the change, I believe, is that Jesus answered that question for the witnesses who wrote the Epistles. In Jesus, God presents a face. Anyone who wonders how God feels about the suffering on this groaning planet need only look at that face. James, Peter, and John had followed Jesus long enough for his facial expressions to be permanently etched on their minds. By watching Jesus respond to a hemorrhaging woman, a grieving centurion, a widow's dead son, an epileptic boy, an old blind man, they learned how God felt about suffering. By no means did Jesus solve the "problem of pain"—he healed only a few in one small corner of the globe—but he did provide an answer to the question, *Does God care?*

Three times that we know of, suffering drove Jesus to tears. He wept when his friend Lazarus died—which gives me a strong clue into how God must feel about my family members and friends who die.

Another time, Jesus sorrowed when he looked out over Jerusalem and realized the fate awaiting that fabled city. "O

Jerusalem, Jerusalem, you who kill the prophets and stone those sent to you, how often I have longed to gather your children together, as a hen gathers her chicks under her wings, but you were not willing," he sighed at one point (Matthew 23:37), using an image he must have drawn from rural Galilee. After fire races through a barn, a farmer may find the corpses of scorched hens, wings outstretched, lying on the barn floor. The farmer kicks aside the corpse, and out scramble tiny chicks. The mother has protected them from the fire, sacrificing her own life in the process. That is what Jesus yearned for: to take the punishment vicariously for his people.

Finally, Hebrews tells us (5:7), Jesus "offered up loud cries and tears to the one who could save him from death." But of course he was not saved from death. In Gethsemane and at Calvary we get the incredible scene that Martin Luther has described as "God struggling with God." Is it too much to suggest that Jesus himself asked the questions that haunt me, that haunt most of us at one time or another. *Do I matter? Does God care?* What else can be the meaning of his quotation from Psalm 22, "My God, my God, why have you forsaken me?"

When Jesus Christ faced pain, he responded much as anyone else does. He did not pray in the garden, "Oh, Lord, I am so grateful that you have chosen me to suffer on your behalf—I rejoice in the privilege!" No, he experienced sorrow, fear, abandonment, and something approaching desperation: " … if it is possible, may this cup be taken from me." Ever attentive to bodily detail, Luke adds, "And being in anguish, he prayed more earnestly, and his sweat was like drops of blood falling to the ground."

We may not get the answer to the problem of pain that we want from Jesus. We get instead the mysterious confirmation that God suffers with us. We are not alone. Jesus bodily reconstructs trust in God. Because of Jesus, I can trust that God truly understands my condition. I can trust that I matter to God, and that God cares, regardless of how things look at the time. When

I begin to doubt, I turn again to the face of Jesus, and there I see the compassionate love of a God well acquainted with grief.

Why Doesn't God Act?

At certain moments in the Israelites' history the question, *Why doesn't God act?* would never have occurred to them. Consider the crowd Moses addressed in the book of Deuteronomy, for example. Raised in the Sinai wilderness, with miraculous provision of food and water fresh in their memory, and visible evidence of God's presence hovering in a cloud before them, they probably did not ponder such a question. If they did, Moses and the few remaining senior citizens would quickly remind them of the ten plagues, the parting of the Red Sea, and the defeat of the mighty Egyptian army.

Yet, scroll back a few years and you find an entire race of doubters, including Moses himself. For four centuries—to get the perspective, think of all that has transpired in world history since Queen Elizabeth's day, before the Pilgrims first set sail for America—they had cried out to God about the terrible conditions in Egypt. God's "chosen people" were a byword among the nations, mere slaves to be exploited at Pharaoh's whim. How many times had the Hebrews cried out, "Why don't you act, God?" before Moses finally arrived on the scene to challenge their doubt?

The prophet Elijah faced a similar crowd of doubters and silenced all their questions with a pyrotechnic display on Mt. Carmel. Yet later he too cowered in a cave, wondering why God didn't simply dispose of King Ahab and his brutal wife, Jezebel. Other prophets, among them the esteemed Isaiah and Jeremiah, must have looked back with envy on Elijah, who had at least a few moments of undisputed glory. The Bible records no miracles by these "prophets of the word," and many ended up martyred for their efforts.

Malachi is the last Old Testament voice, and his book serves as a good prelude to the next four hundred years of biblical silence. From the Israelites' point of view, those four centuries could be termed "the era of lowered expectations." They had returned to the land after the Babylonian captivity, but that land remained a backwater province under the domination of Persia (or Greece, or Rome—imperial armies took turns tramping through Israel). The newly reconstructed temple was a sad imitation of Solomon's architectural wonder. The grand future of triumph and world peace described by the prophets seemed a distant pipe dream.

A general malaise set in among the Jews, a low-grade disappointment with God that showed in their complaints and also in their actions. As the people expressed it then, "It is futile to serve God. What did we gain by carrying out his requirements . . . ?" That final question troubled the Jews for centuries after Malachi and the remaining prophets had faded from the scene. They saw no miracles, no spectacular interventions, and heard no new words from the Lord. Had God forgotten how to be merciful? Had he plugged his ears against their groans? The Old Testament ends on a note of disappointment, unfulfilled longings, and faint hope.

Jack Miles points out that the arrangement of the Hebrew Bible expresses this longing even more poignantly. The Bible that Christians use proceeds from the Pentateuch through the History books, Poetry, and then Prophets, ending with Malachi. Jews use a different arrangement in the Tanakh. After the Pentateuch (or Torah), they organize their books into the Prophets (including such "history" books as Joshua, Judges, Samuel, and Kings), and then an assortment called "The Writings."

This last section begins with Psalms, then moves on to Proverbs, Job, Song of Songs, Ruth, Lamentations, Ecclesiastes, Esther, Daniel, Ezra, Nehemiah, and the Chronicles. Miles notes that such an arrangement underscores an increasing sense of

God's silence or withdrawal. In fact, after the long speech at the end of Job, God never again speaks. Chronicles repeats some of the speeches God made earlier, usually quoting them verbatim from other books. Song of Songs and Esther never even mention God. Other books refer to God, and include prayers to him. But, after Job, God never speaks again. The years of waiting—the millennia of waiting—descend. If hunger is the best cook, as Luther said, then we arrive at Jesus, at the Old Testament's end, in a famished state.

I have a Jewish friend who sometimes leads tour groups in Israel. He quickly learned that the real money in such tour groups comes from evangelical Christians on pilgrimage to "the Holy Land." It went against his grain to study the details of Jesus' life, for his parents had always forbidden mention of Jesus' name. As he did so, though, and as he got to know Christian tourists who knew more Jewish history than he did, he was struck by an astonishing convergence.

He learned that the conservative Christian groups believed world history was moving toward a culmination in which Israel would play a crucial role. They kept talking about the "second coming" of Jesus, quoting the prophecies he had learned in Hebrew school. As he listened to them, he realized that he and they were waiting for the same thing: a Messiah, a Prince of Peace, to restore justice and peace to a badly fractured planet. The Christians anticipated Messiah's second coming; as a Jew, he was still looking for the first coming. "Wouldn't it be amazing," he once told me, "if we found out we were all waiting for the same person."

To the question, *Why doesn't God act?* Jews and Christians have the same answer, with one crucial difference. Jews believe that God will act, by sending the Messiah. Christians believe that God has acted, by sending the Messiah, and will act once more, by sending him again, this time in power and glory, not in weakness and humility.

Unfinished Business

One night just before Christmas 1988, I sat in the Barbican Center in London listening to a rousing performance of Handel's *Messiah*. I had landed in the morning, bought tickets for a performance that same evening, and fought to stay awake by strolling through downtown London and stopping for coffee every few hours. I hardly anticipated what I got that evening. Something about this concert—my sleep-starved, caffeine-buzzed state, the London setting, the performance itself—transported me back closer, much closer, to Handel's day. The event became, quite unexpectedly, not just a performance but a kind of epiphany, a striking revelation of the entire Christian story. In a manner I had never before experienced, I felt able to see beyond the music to the soul of the piece.

More than any other place in the world, London values theater, and these performers were not merely singing, they were acting out the drama of *Messiah*'s words. As I leaned back in the padded seat and listened to the familiar recitations of *Messiah*, Part 1, it was easy to understand how the oratorio came to be associated with the Advent season (though Handel wrote it for Easter). Handel begins with a collection of lilting prophecies from Isaiah about a coming King who will bring peace and comfort to a disturbed and violent world. The music builds, swelling from a solo tenor ("Comfort ye my people ...") to a full chorus joyously celebrating the day when "the glory of the Lord shall be revealed."

Any listener, no matter how musically naive, can sense an ominous change at the beginning of Part 2. Handel telegraphs the darkening mood with dense orchestral chords in a minor key. Part 2 describes the world's response to the Messiah, and the story is tragic beyond all telling. Handel relies mostly on the words of Isaiah 52–53, that remarkably vivid account written centuries before Jesus' birth.

All sound ceases for a moment, and after this dramatic pause the contralto, with no accompaniment, gives the disturbing news: "He was de-spis-ed ... re-ject-ed." She pronounces each syllable with great effort, as if the facts of history are too painful to recite. Violins moodily repeat each musical phrase.

At Calvary, history hung suspended. The bright hopes that had swirled around the long-awaited deliverer of Israel collapsed in darkness that fateful night. Dangling like a scarecrow between two thieves, the Messiah provoked at worst derision, at best pity. "All they that see him laugh him to scorn," says the tenor, who then adds, in the most poignant moment of Handel's oratorio, "*Behold,* and see if there be any sorrow like unto his sorrow."

Yet all is not lost! A few measures later that tenor, the same one who cried out in abject despair, introduces the first glimmer of hope in *Messiah,* Part 2: "But thou didst not leave his soul in hell." Almost immediately the entire chorus takes up the shout of joy, for the defeat at Calvary was only an *apparent* defeat. The scarecrow corpse did not remain a corpse. He was the King of Glory after all.

"Hallelujah!" the chorus cries out at last, and from there the music soars into what is unarguably the most famous portion of Handel's *Messiah,* and one of the most jubilant passages of music ever composed. Handel himself said that when he wrote the Hallelujah Chorus, "I did think I did see all Heaven before me, and the Great God himself." "King of Kings ... Lord of Lords ... reign for ever and ever"—Handel gives each phrase the resplendent fugal development it merits. When King George I heard the Hallelujah Chorus at the London premiere in 1742, he, the nation's sovereign, stood to his feet in amazement, and audiences have honored his respectful tribute ever since.

Some skeptics suggest that King George stood to his feet less out of respect than out of the mistaken assumption that Handel's *Messiah* had reached its conclusion with the Hallelujah Chorus. Even today novices in the audience make the same mistake. Who can blame them? After two hours of performance, the music seems to come to a point of culmination in the exuberant Chorus. What more is needed?

I had never really considered the question until that night at the Barbican Center. But as I glanced at the few paragraphs of libretto remaining, my eyes still burning from lack of sleep, I realized what was missing from *Messiah*, Parts 1 and 2. My Jewish friend who leads tour groups in Israel is right in one important respect: Jesus of Nazareth did not come close to fulfilling the soaring predictions of the prophets. "Glory to God in the highest, and on earth peace, good will toward men," cried the angels who announced Jesus' birth. Have peace and good will filled the earth since Jesus' birth? A visit to his homeland will quickly disabuse that notion.

When my wife and I flew to England earlier that day, the route took us over the polar icecap, which even at night could be seen glowing 30,000 feet below us during the season of the midnight sun. I knew that beneath the icecap, nuclear attack submarines prowled, each one capable of killing a hundred million people. We landed in London to the news that a train had crashed, killing fifty-one commuters; newspapers were full of photos of the carnage. Within the week, a terrorist bombed Pan Am flight 103 over Lockerbie, Scotland, killing 270. Is this the world God had in mind at Creation? The world Jesus had in mind at Incarnation?

For reasons such as these, Handel's *Messiah* could not rightly end with the Hallelujah Chorus. The Messiah has come in "glory" (Part 1); the Messiah has died and been resurrected (Part 2). Why, then, does the world remain in such a sorry state? Handel's Part 3 attempts an answer. Beyond the images from Bethlehem and Calvary, the music reaches for a more messianic image: Jesus as Sovereign Lord. The Incarnation did not usher in the end of history—only the beginning of the end. Much work remains before creation is restored to God's original intent.

In a brilliant stroke, Part 3 of *Messiah* opens with a quotation from Job, that tragic figure who clung stubbornly to faith amid circumstances that called for bleak despair. "I know that my Redeemer liveth, and that He shall stand at the latter day upon the earth," the soprano sings out. Overwhelmed by personal tragedy, with scant evidence of a sovereign God, Job still managed to believe—and, Handel implies, so should we.

From that defiant opening, *Messiah,* Part 3, shifts to the apostle Paul's reflections on Christ's death and then moves quickly to his lofty words about a final resurrection ("The trumpet shall sound, and the dead shall be raised . . ."). Christ's death and bodily resurrection represented at once a decisive defeat of evil and an "advance echo" of what will someday happen to all who are in him. God has acted once, by joining us on this groaning planet. God will act again, by returning in power and glory to restore it to its original design.

Just as the tragedy of Good Friday was transformed into the triumph of Easter Sunday, one day all war, all violence, all injustice, all sadness will likewise be transformed. Then and only then will we be able to say, "O death, where is thy sting? O grave, where is thy victory?" Only then will the urgent questions from the Old Testament resolve. *Do we matter? Does God care?* We must live in faith, aware that those questions will lack a final answer until that decisive day when God does act, spectacularly, in Jesus' Second Coming.

Writers of the Old Testament looked back, at the God of the covenant who had expressed his love for his people so many times, and also forward, to the time when God would send a deliverer. Those of us who come later also have a double vision. We look back to the first coming of Jesus, and see unmistakable proof that individuals matter to the God of the Universe, and proof that God cares. We continue to look forward, though, to the Creator's unfinished business, to the as-yet-unfulfilled promises of the prophets.

Handel's masterwork ends with a single scene frozen in time. To make his point about the Christ of eternity, the librettist could have settled on the scene from Revelation 2, where Jesus appears with a face like the shining sun and eyes like blazing fire. Instead, his text concludes with the scene from Revelation 4–5, perhaps the most vivid image in a book of vivid imagery. That passage foretells the consummation of all history.

Twenty-four impressive rulers are gathered together, along with four living creatures who represent the mightiest among birds, domestic animals, wild beasts, and humans—the best in all creation. These creatures and rulers kneel respectfully before a throne luminous with lightning and encircled by a rainbow. An angel asks who is worthy to break a seal that will open up the scroll of history? In other words, who is worthy to bring history to its appropriate conclusion? Neither the creatures nor the twenty-four rulers are worthy. The author realizes well the significance of that moment: "I wept and wept because no one was found who was worthy to open the scroll or look inside."

In addition to these creatures, impotent for the grand task, one more creature stands before the gleaming throne. Though appearance offers little to recommend him, he is nevertheless history's sole remaining hope. "Then I saw a Lamb, looking as if it had been slain. . . ." A lamb! A helpless lamb, and a slaughtered one at that. Yet John in Revelation, and Handel in *Messiah*, sum up all history in this one mysterious image. The great God who became a baby, who became a lamb, who became a sacrifice—this God, who bore our stripes and died our death, this one alone is worthy. That is where Handel leaves us, with the great "Worthy is the Lamb" chorus, followed by exultant Amens.

Amens from the Westminster Choir were still echoing throughout the large hall as I looked around and asked myself another question: What percentage of these sophisticated Londoners, now applauding so lustily, understand its meaning?

What percentage believe it? Parts 1 and 2 of *Messiah* they could probably assent to: in this once-Christian land, few would openly deny the historical facts of Jesus' birth and crucifixion.

Part 3, however, is the stumbling block. We were sitting in a modern brick-and-oak auditorium in the late twentieth century in a materialistic culture light-years removed from the imagery of slaughtered lambs. But Handel understood that history and civilization are not what they appear. Auditoriums, cultures, civilizations all rise and fall. History has proved beyond doubt that nothing fashioned by the hand of humanity will last. We need something greater than history, something outside history. We need a Lamb slain before the foundation of the world.

I confess that belief in an invisible world, a world beyond this one, does not come easily for me. Like many moderns, I sometimes wonder if reality ends with the material world around us, if life ends at death, if history ends with annihilation or solar exhaustion. But that evening I had no such doubts.

Jet lag and fatigue had produced in me something akin to an out-of-body state, and for that moment the grand tapestry woven by Handel's music seemed more real by far than my everyday world. I felt I had a glimpse of the grand sweep of cosmic history. All of it centered on the Messiah who came on a rescue mission, who died on that mission, and who wrought from that death the salvation of the world. I went away with renewed belief that he—and we—shall indeed reign forever and ever. In that day the questions that so plagued the Old Testament writers, and still plague many of us today, will seem like distant memories, the kinds of questions a child might ask.

ABOUT THE AUTHOR

Philip Yancey serves as editor-at-large for *Christianity Today* magazine. He has written eleven Gold Medallion Award-winning books, including *Where Is God When It Hurts? Disappointment with God, The Bible Jesus Read,* and *The Gift of Pain.* His books *The Jesus I Never Knew* and *What's So Amazing About Grace?* were also awarded the Christian Book of the Year. He is also the author of *Reaching for the Invisible God.*

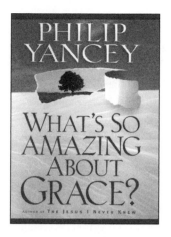

What's So Amazing About Grace?
Philip Yancey

We speak of grace often. But do we understand it? More important, do we truly believe in it . . . and do our lives proclaim it as powerfully as our words?

In *What's So Amazing About Grace?* award-winning author Philip Yancey explores grace at street level. If grace is God's love for the undeserving, he asks, then what does it look like in action? And if Christians are its sole dispensers, then how are we doing at lavishing grace on a world that knows far more of cruelty and unforgiveness than it does of merecy?

Yancey sets grace in the midst of life's stark images, tests its mettle against horrific "ungrace". Can grace survive in the midst of such atrocities as the Nazi holocaust? Can it triumph over the brutality of the Ku Klux Klan? Grace does not excuse sin, says Yancey, but it treasures the sinner.

In his most personal and provocative book ever, Yancey offers compelling, true portraits of grace's life-changing power. He searches for its presence in his own life and in the church. He asks, How can Christians contend graciously with moral issues that threaten all they hold dear? And he challenges us to become living answers to a world that desperately wants to know, *What's So Amazing About Grace?*

Pick up a copy today at your favorite bookstore!

Hardcover 0-310-21327-4
Softcover 0-310-24565-6
Study Guide 0-310-21904-3
Audio Pages® Abridged Cassettes 0-310-21578-1
Audio Pages® Unabridged Cassettes 0-310-23228-7
Zondervan*Groupware*™ 0-310-23323-2
Leader's Guide 0-310-23326-7
Participant's Guide 0-310-23325-9

ZONDERVAN™

GRAND RAPIDS, MICHIGAN 49530
WWW.ZONDERVAN.COM

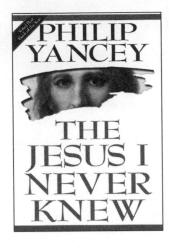

The Jesus I Never Knew
Philip Yancey

What happens when a respected Christian journalist decides to put his preconceptions aside and take a long look at the Jesus described in the Gospels? How does the Jesus of the New Testament compare to the "new, rediscovered" Jesus—or even the Jesus we think we know so well? Best-selling author Philip Yancey says, "The Jesus I got to know in writing this book is very different from the Jesus I learned about in Sunday school. In some ways he is more comforting; in some ways more terrifying."

Yancey offers a new and different perspective on the life of Christ and his work—his teaching, his miracle, his death and resurrection—and ultimately, who he was and why he came. Relating the gospel events to the world we live in today, *The Jesus I Never Knew* gives a moving and refreshing portrait of the central figure of history. With a willingness to tackle difficult questions, Yancey looks at the radical words of this itinerant Jewish carpenter and asks whether we are taking him seriously enough in our own day and age.

From the manger in Bethlehem to the cross in Jerusalem, Yancey presents a complex character who generates questions as well as answers; a disturbing and exhilarating Jesus who wants to radically transform your life and stretch your faith.

Pick up a copy today at your favorite bookstore!

Hardcover 0-310-38570-9
Softcover 0-310-21923-X
Study Guide 0-310-21805-5
Audio Pages® Abridged Cassettes 0-310-20418-6
Audio Pages® Unabridged Cassettes 0-310-23227-9
Zondervan*Groupware*™ 0-310-22358-X
Leader's Guide 0-310-22432-2
Participant's Guide 0-310-22433-0

GRAND RAPIDS, MICHIGAN 49530
WWW.ZONDERVAN.COM

Where Is God When It Hurts?
Philip Yancey

"If there is a loving God, then why is it that . . ." You've heard that question, perhaps asked it yourself. No matter how you complete it, at its root lies the issue of pain. Does God order our suffering? Does he decree an abusive childhood, orchestrate a jet crash, steer a tornado through a community? Or did he simply wind up the world's mainspring and now is watching from a distance?

In this Gold Medallion Award-winning book, Philip Yancey reveals a God who is neither capricious nor unconcerned. Using examples from the Bible and from his own experiences, Yancey looks at pain—physical, emotional, and spiritual—and helps us understand why we suffer. This most current edition of what is perhaps Yancey's best-known book will speak to those for whom life sometimes just doesn't make sense. And it will help equip anyone who wants to reach out to someone in pain but just doesn't know what to say.

Softcover 0-310-24572-9
Mass Market 0-310-21437-8

Disappointment with God

Three Questions No One Asks Aloud

Philip Yancey

Is God Unfair?

Is God Silent?

Is God Hidden?

These questions are asked with piercing honesty and biblical certainty. Step by step, Philip Yancey retraces the long journey toward understanding the answers to these and other questions. If God desires our love, why does he sometimes put obstacles in the way? Why does he seem so distant? What can we expect from him after all?

No part of the Bible goes unstudied in the author's search for God's hidden nature in this compelling and profound book. A Gold Medallion Award winner, *Disappointment with God* has had an overwhelming impact on many lives—it can change yours.

Softcover 0-310-51781-8
Mass Market 0-310-21436-X

Pick up a copy at your favorite bookstore today!

ZONDERVAN™

GRAND RAPIDS, MICHIGAN 49530

WWW.ZONDERVAN.COM

Church: Why Bother?

My Personal Pilgrimage

Philip Yancey

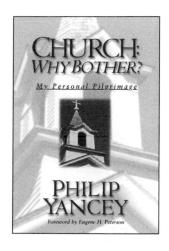

Philip Yancey asks the question that haunts many believers: Why should I bother with the church? From growing up in rural Georgia in a fundamentalist church to his experience at LaSalle Street Church in inner city Chicago, he reflects on the church, his own perceptions of it, and the various metaphors the Bible uses to describe it. Yancey's own early church experience set his faith back by many years. In *Church: Why Bother?* he offers us a glimpse of his pilgrimage back to faith and to the church as a place of real community and spiritual vitality.

In this candid, thought-provoking account, he reveals the reasons behind his own journey back from skepticism to wholehearted participation in the church, and weighs the church's human failings against its compelling excellencies as the body of Christ.

Softcover 0-310-24313-0

Pick up a copy at your favorite bookstore today!

ZONDERVAN™

GRAND RAPIDS, MICHIGAN 49530

WWW.ZONDERVAN.COM

Meet the Bible

*A Panorama of God's Word in
366 Daily Readings and Reflections*

Philip Yancey

Brenda Quinn

The story of the Bible starts with the simple statement, "In the beginning, God created . . ." From that first sentence of Genesis, the story of salvation unfolds in strange and wonderful mingling of the commonplace and the miraculous, the human and the transcendent. But if you were born after the baby boom, chances are the Bible seems more like an item of passing interest than a book of depth and meaning for the twenty-first century. If you're not familiar with the Bible, it can be difficult to put into perspective the puzzle of kings and prophets, giants and seven-headed dragons, shepherd boys and itinerant preachers, Old Testament law and New Testament grace.

Meet the Bible introduces you to the full, epic sweep of the Bible—the characters, the places, the times, the stories, and the meanings of this Book of books—and shows you that even the most obscure passage can hold relevance for your life once you understand what to look for. Award-winning writer Philip Yancey and author Brenda Quinn are your guides on this one-year reading tour of the Bible. Each day's reading includes Scripture, contemporary commentary, and questions for contemplation—all designed to offer insight into how the passage fits into the overall story of the Bible, and how it can speak to your life today.

Hardcover 0-310-22776-3   Softcover 0-310-24303-3

Pick up a copy at your favorite bookstore today!

ZONDERVAN™

GRAND RAPIDS, MICHIGAN 49530

WWW.ZONDERVAN.COM

Fearfully and Wonderfully Made
Philip Yancey
Dr. Paul Brand

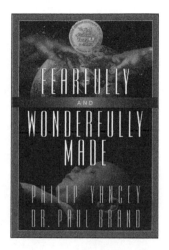

Mysterious, intricate, pulsing with energy . . . the human body is an endlessly fascinating repository of secrets. The miracle of the skin, the strength and structure of the bones, the dynamic balance of the muscles . . .your physical being is knit according to a pattern of incredible purpose. In *Fearfully and Wonderfully Made,* renowned surgeon Dr. Paul Brand and best-selling writer Philip Yancey explore the human body. Join them in a remarkable journey through inner space—a spellbinding world of cells, systems, and chemistry that bears the impress of a still deeper, unseen reality. This Gold Medallion Award-winning book uncovers eternal statements that God has made in the very structure of our bodies, presenting captivating insights into the Body of Christ.

Softcover 0-310-35451-X

Pick up a copy at your favorite bookstore today!

ZONDERVAN™

GRAND RAPIDS, MICHIGAN 49530
WWW.ZONDERVAN.COM

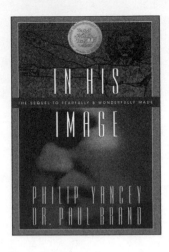

In His Image
Philip Yancey
Dr. Paul Brand

The voice of God is a heartbeat away...

This companion book to *Fearfully and Wonderfully Made,* skillfully coauthored by award-winning writer Philip Yancey, unfolds spiritual truths through a physician's knowledge of the blood, the head, the spirit, and pain.

In *Fearfully and Wonderfully Made,* Philip Yancey and Dr. Paul Brand revealed how God's voice is encoded in the very structure of our bodies. *In His Image* takes up where its predecessor left off, beckoning us once again inward and onward to fresh exploration and discovery.

Yancey and Brand show how accurately and intricately the human body portrays the Body of Christ. In five sections—Image, Blood, Head, Spirit, and Pain—the acclaimed surgeon and the award-winning writer unlock the remarkable, living lessons contained in our physical makeup. This Gold Medallion Award-winning book will open your eyes to the complex miracle of the human body, and the even more compelling spiritual truths that it reflects.

Pick up a copy at your favorite bookstore today!

ZONDERVAN™

GRAND RAPIDS, MICHIGAN 49530

WWW.ZONDERVAN.COM